I0427263

Escape the 9-to-5

Build Your Fortune with Proven Options Trading Strategies

-

Transform Your Life with Smart Investments and Financial Savvy

By

Ernie Braveboy

Table of Contents

Preface

In today's fast-paced world, the traditional 9-to-5 work structure no longer guarantees the financial security or personal freedom it once did. Many of us dream of breaking free from this cycle, longing for a life where our time and income are not directly tied to the hours we spend in an office. It was this very aspiration that set me on the path of exploring the financial markets, leading me to the world of options trading—a realm where flexibility meets opportunity.

Options trading, often viewed as complex and risky, is misunderstood by many. Yet, with the right knowledge and strategy, it can be an incredibly powerful tool for building wealth. My journey into this field was not without its challenges. I encountered my share of losses and setbacks, each teaching me valuable lessons. These experiences, both good and bad, have been distilled into this book, aimed at demystifying options trading for beginners.

This book is not just a guide; it's a bridge to a new way of thinking about income and investment. It's written with the hope that it will empower you to take that first step towards financial independence, armed with knowledge and confidence. Whether you're looking to supplement your income, save for retirement, or transition to trading full-time, this book will lay the groundwork for your success.

The strategies and insights shared here are the culmination of years of learning, trading, and teaching others. They are designed to be accessible, practical, and actionable. By turning these pages, you embark on a journey not just to understand options trading, but to transform your financial future.

Welcome to the first step of your trading journey. Let's break free from the 9-to-5 together.

Ernie Braveboy

Acknowledgments

Writing this book has been a journey—a confluence of personal experience, countless hours of research, and the wisdom shared by many. It's a journey that, while embarked upon alone, was made possible through the support, guidance, and encouragement of numerous individuals to whom I owe my heartfelt thanks.

First and foremost, I extend my deepest gratitude to my family. Their unwavering support and belief in my vision have been the bedrock of my perseverance. To my partner, whose patience and understanding made the long hours of writing and research not only bearable but enjoyable, I am eternally grateful.

I owe a debt of gratitude to my mentors in the trading community. Their insights and guidance have been invaluable, shaping not only my trading strategies but also the way I perceive the markets. Their willingness to share their knowledge and experience has been a beacon of light on my path.

To my peers and colleagues, whose constructive feedback and challenging questions pushed me to delve deeper and think harder, I am thankful. Their perspectives have enriched this work in countless ways.

Special thanks go to my early readers, whose enthusiasm and constructive criticism were instrumental in refining this manuscript. Their engagement and feedback helped me to clarify complex ideas and ensure the practical applicability of the strategies discussed.

I must also acknowledge the countless authors and researchers in the field of finance and trading whose works have informed and inspired me. Their contributions to the field have laid the foundations upon which this book is built.

Lastly, to you, the reader, for choosing to embark on this journey with me. Your desire to learn and grow is the ultimate inspiration for this work. It is my sincere hope that this book serves as a valuable tool in your pursuit of financial independence and success in options trading.

Ernie Braveboy

Introduction: The Journey from 9-to-5 to Financial Freedom

For many of us, the 9-to-5 job is more than just a routine; it's a symbol of security and stability. But in the quiet moments, between the rush of deadlines and the daily commute, a question lingers: Is there more to life than this? This book was born out of that question and the journey it sparked—a journey from the predictability of a salaried job to the dynamic world of options trading, a realm where the potential for financial freedom and personal autonomy beckons.

Options trading, with its intricate strategies and potential for significant returns, might seem daunting at first glance. It's a field often shrouded in jargon, complex charts, and the high-stakes stories that pepper financial news. Yet, beneath this veneer lies a structured, accessible path to financial independence for those willing to learn its intricacies.

This book is your guide on that path. It's designed not just for those looking to escape the 9-to-5 grind but for anyone who dreams of a life where their time and financial well-being are not at the mercy of a traditional job. The strategies and insights within these pages are distilled from years of trading experience, countless successes and failures, and the collective wisdom of a community of traders who have found their freedom in the markets.

The journey from 9-to-5 to financial freedom is as much about mindset as it is about strategy. It requires a shift from seeking security in a job to finding stability in knowledge, skill, and the ability to navigate the markets. This book aims to equip you with that knowledge and skill, breaking down complex concepts into understandable, actionable steps.

As you turn these pages, you'll explore the fundamentals of options trading, from the basics of calls and puts to advanced strategies that can help you maximize your returns while managing risk. You'll learn not just the mechanics of trading but also the critical thinking and discipline required to succeed.

But this book is more than a manual on options trading. It's an invitation to challenge the status quo, to dare to envision a life where your financial destiny is in your own hands. Whether you're looking to supplement your income, save for the future, or transition to trading full-time, the journey starts here.

Let's embark on this journey together, from the familiar shores of the 9-to-5 to the vast, uncharted waters of financial freedom. The path may be challenging, but the rewards— autonomy, financial independence, and the fulfillment of personal potential—are immeasurable.

Welcome to your new beginning.

Ernie Braveboy

Chapter 1: The World of Options Trading

Introduction

Welcome to the world of options trading, a fascinating realm within the financial markets where flexibility, strategy, and opportunity converge. Unlike traditional stock trading, options offer a unique set of advantages and challenges, making them an attractive tool for investors seeking to enhance their portfolio, hedge against market volatility, or capitalize on market movements without committing large amounts of capital upfront.

This chapter serves as your gateway into the intricacies of options trading. We'll demystify the jargon, break down the basics, and lay the foundation upon which you can build your trading knowledge and skills. Whether you're a complete novice or someone with a bit of trading experience looking to expand your repertoire, this chapter is designed to provide you with a solid understanding of what options are, how they work, and why they're a valuable addition to any trader's arsenal.

1.1 What Are Options?

At its core, an option is a contract that gives the buyer the right, but not the obligation, to buy or sell an underlying asset at a predetermined price within a specified time frame. This fundamental concept is crucial to understanding the flexibility and potential of options trading. We'll explore the two primary types of options—calls and puts—and illustrate how they can be used for various trading strategies.

1.2 The Players in the Options Market

The options market is made up of buyers and sellers, each with their own strategies, goals, and risk tolerances. Understanding the roles and perspectives of these market participants is key to navigating the options trading landscape effectively. We'll introduce you to the market makers, the retail traders, and the institutional investors, and explain how their interactions shape the market dynamics.

1.3 How Options Work

Options trading is often praised for its flexibility, but with that flexibility comes complexity. In this section, we'll break down the mechanics of how options work, including the key concepts of strike price, expiration date, and intrinsic vs. extrinsic value. By the end of this section, you'll have a clear understanding of the factors that influence an option's price and how to read an options chain—a crucial skill for any trader.

1.4 Types of Options

While calls and puts are the most basic types of options, the world of options trading is vast and varied. We'll delve into the different types of options available to traders, including American vs. European options, index options, and exotic options, highlighting their unique characteristics and suitable trading scenarios.

1.5 Why Trade Options?

Options trading offers numerous advantages, from leverage and risk management to strategic diversity and income generation. This section will outline the key benefits of incorporating options into your trading strategy, backed by practical examples and comparisons to other forms of trading.

1.6 Risks and Considerations

While the potential rewards of options trading are significant, so too are the risks. It's crucial for traders to be aware of these risks and to understand the factors that can impact the success of their trades. We'll discuss the common pitfalls and challenges associated with options trading and provide tips for managing risk and avoiding costly mistakes.

Conclusion

As we wrap up this introductory chapter, you'll have gained a solid foundation in the basics of options trading. Armed with this knowledge, you'll be better prepared to delve deeper into the strategies and techniques that can help you navigate the options market successfully. Remember, the journey to becoming a proficient options trader is a marathon, not a sprint. Patience, continuous learning, and disciplined practice are your keys to success.

In the next chapter, we'll build on this foundation by exploring how to set the stage for successful trading, including selecting the right trading platform, understanding the regulatory environment, and developing the mindset necessary for trading success.

1.1 What Are Options?

Options are financial instruments that belong to a broader category known as derivatives. This is because their value is derived from the value of an underlying asset, which can be stocks, indexes, commodities, or even currency rates. An option itself is a contract between two parties: the buyer and the seller. This contract offers the buyer the right, but not the obligation, to buy (in the case of a call option) or sell (in the case of a put option) the underlying asset at a predetermined price, known as the strike price, within a specific time period.

The Essence of Options

To truly understand options, it's essential to grasp two fundamental concepts: the call option and the put option.

- **Call Options**: Buying a call option gives you the right to purchase the underlying asset at the strike price before the option expires. Traders buy call options when they anticipate the price of the underlying asset will rise, allowing them to buy the asset at a price lower than the market value.
- **Put Options**: Conversely, buying a put option gives you the right to sell the underlying asset at the strike price before the option expires. Put options are typically purchased when traders expect the price of the underlying asset to decline, enabling them to sell the asset at a price higher than the market value.

Options Terminology

Understanding options requires familiarity with the specific terminology used in the trading world:

- **Strike Price**: The price at which the option holder can buy (call) or sell (put) the underlying asset.
- **Expiration Date**: The date on which the option expires and can no longer be exercised.
- **Premium**: The price paid by the buyer to the seller to acquire the option. This price is influenced by various factors including the underlying asset's price, time to expiration, and volatility.
- **In-the-Money (ITM)**: An option is "in-the-money" if exercising it would result in a profit. For call options, this means the underlying asset's price is above the strike price. For put options, it's when the asset's price is below the strike price.
- **Out-of-the-Money (OTM)**: An option is "out-of-the-money" if exercising it would not be profitable. For call options, this is when the underlying asset's price is below the strike price. For put options, it's when the asset's price is above the strike price.
- **At-the-Money (ATM)**: An option is "at-the-money" if the underlying asset's price is equal to the strike price.

Why Options?

Options trading offers several strategic advantages, including leverage, flexibility, and risk management. With options, traders can control a significant amount of the underlying asset with a relatively small investment (the premium). This leverage can amplify returns but also magnifies risk, making it crucial to understand options thoroughly before trading.

Options also provide a degree of flexibility not found in other financial instruments. They allow traders to speculate on both the rise and fall of market prices and to hedge against potential losses in other investments.

Conclusion

Options are a versatile and complex tool in the financial markets, offering opportunities for strategic trading and investment. However, the very features that make options attractive—leverage and flexibility—also introduce significant risk. Understanding the fundamentals of options, including the types of options and key terminology, is essential for anyone looking to navigate the options market successfully. As we progress through this book, we'll delve deeper into strategies, risk management, and practical applications to help you build a solid foundation in options trading.

1.2 Why Trade Options?

Options trading, with its unique characteristics and flexibility, offers a plethora of advantages to the savvy investor. Whether you're looking to hedge your investment portfolio, generate income, or speculate on stock price movements with limited risk, options can be a powerful tool in your financial arsenal. This section explores the key reasons why traders opt for options and how these financial instruments can complement various investment strategies.

Leverage and Capital Efficiency

One of the most compelling reasons to trade options is leverage. Leverage allows you to control a larger amount of the underlying asset with a relatively small investment (the premium paid for the option). This means that with a smaller upfront capital, you can achieve a significant exposure to the price movements of the underlying asset, potentially leading to amplified profits compared to investing directly in the asset. However, it's crucial to remember that while leverage can magnify returns, it also increases potential losses.

Risk Management and Hedging

Options are invaluable tools for managing risk in your investment portfolio. By using options, investors can protect their holdings against adverse price movements. For example, purchasing put options on stocks you own (a strategy known as a protective put) can act as an insurance policy, limiting potential losses if the stock price falls dramatically. This hedging capability allows investors to mitigate risk while maintaining exposure to potential upside.

Flexibility and Strategic Diversity

The versatility of options trading strategies is unmatched. Options enable traders to profit from not just upward or downward price movements but also sideways and volatile markets. Strategies range from simple to complex and can be tailored to fit various market outlooks and risk tolerances. Whether you're bullish, bearish, or neutral on the market or a particular stock, there's an options strategy designed to align with your forecast and risk profile.

Income Generation

Options also offer opportunities for income generation through strategies such as writing covered calls. This strategy involves selling call options on stocks you already own, providing you with immediate income in the form of premiums received. While this strategy can limit the upside potential if the stock's price rises above the strike price of the call option, it can be an effective way to generate steady income from your stock holdings, especially in flat or mildly bullish markets.

Cost Efficiency

Trading options can be more cost-efficient than buying the underlying asset outright. Since you're only purchasing the right to buy or sell the asset at a specific price, the capital outlay is typically lower than acquiring the asset itself. This cost efficiency makes options an attractive choice for investors looking to gain exposure to high-priced stocks or assets without committing significant capital.

Speculation with Limited Risk

Options allow for speculation on the direction of stock prices with a well-defined risk profile. When buying options, the most you can lose is the premium paid, offering a clear risk limit. This predefined risk is particularly appealing for speculative strategies, where the potential for high returns is balanced against the certainty of limited loss.

Conclusion

The allure of options trading lies in its ability to offer leverage, risk management, strategic flexibility, income generation, and cost efficiency, all within a framework of controlled risk. However, the complexities and risks associated with options trading necessitate a thorough understanding and careful strategy implementation. As we delve deeper into the mechanics of options trading in the following chapters, keep these advantages in mind as the foundation upon which we'll build more advanced strategies and techniques.

1.3 Understanding Calls and Puts

Calls and puts are the fundamental building blocks of options trading. Mastery of these concepts is essential for anyone looking to navigate the options market. This section will delve into the mechanics, uses, and strategies associated with call and put options, providing a solid foundation for both novice and experienced traders to build upon.

Call Options: The Right to Buy

A call option grants the holder the right, but not the obligation, to buy a specified quantity of an underlying asset at a predetermined price (the strike price) within a fixed period. Investors buy call options when they anticipate the price of the underlying asset will rise before the option expires. The appeal of a call option lies in its leverage potential; it enables traders to benefit from price increases in the underlying asset while limiting their risk to the premium paid for the option.

Key Characteristics of Call Options:

- **Leverage**: Control a larger amount of the underlying asset with a smaller upfront investment.
- **Profit Potential**: Unlimited upside potential as the market price of the underlying asset rises.
- **Risk**: Limited to the premium paid for the option.

Put Options: The Right to Sell

Conversely, a put option gives the holder the right, but not the obligation, to sell a specified quantity of an underlying asset at a strike price within a certain time frame. Put options are typically purchased as a form of insurance against a decline in the price of the underlying asset or as a speculative play to profit from expected downward price movements. The put option serves as a hedge, offering protection by allowing the holder to sell the underlying asset at the strike price, even if the market price falls significantly below that level.

Key Characteristics of Put Options:

- **Protection**: Acts as a form of insurance for existing holdings in the underlying asset.
- **Profit from Declines**: Enables traders to profit from decreases in the underlying asset's price.
- **Risk**: Limited to the premium paid for the option, if held to expiration.

Exercising Options

The decision to exercise an option depends on the relationship between the strike price and the market price of the underlying asset. For call options, if the market price exceeds the strike price (in-the-money), the holder can buy the asset at the lower strike price, potentially selling it immediately at the market price for a profit. For put options, if the market price falls below the strike price (in-the-money), the holder can sell the asset at the higher strike price.

However, most options are not exercised but are instead traded or allowed to expire. The value of an option is not just in its intrinsic value (the difference between the strike price and the market price) but also in its time value—the potential for the market price to move favorably before expiration.

Strategies Involving Calls and Puts

Calls and puts can be used in various strategies, from straightforward buying and selling to more complex trades like spreads, straddles, and combinations. Some basic strategies include:

- **Buying Calls/Puts**: Straightforward strategy for speculating on the direction of the underlying asset's price with limited risk.
- **Covered Call Writing**: Involves holding the underlying asset and selling a call option on it to generate income, with the trade-off of capping the upside potential.
- **Protective Puts**: Buying a put option as a form of insurance for an existing holding in the underlying asset, protecting against significant declines.

Conclusion

Understanding calls and puts is fundamental to options trading, offering traders a range of strategies for speculation, income generation, and risk management. As we progress through this book, we'll explore these strategies in greater detail, equipping you with the knowledge to leverage calls and puts effectively in your trading endeavors.

1.4 The Options Market: How It Works

The options market is a dynamic component of the financial markets, where participants trade options contracts on various underlying assets. Understanding how the options market works is crucial for traders aiming to navigate it successfully. This section will explore the structure of the options market, the roles of its participants, and the mechanisms that underpin options trading.

Structure of the Options Market

The options market consists of two main segments: the exchange-traded options market and the over-the-counter (OTC) options market.

- **Exchange-Traded Options**: These options are standardized contracts that trade on regulated exchanges. They have fixed strike prices, expiration dates, and contract sizes. Exchange-traded options provide liquidity, transparency, and regulatory oversight, making them a popular choice for individual and institutional investors alike.
- **Over-the-Counter (OTC) Options**: OTC options are customized contracts traded directly between two parties, without going through a public exchange. These options can be tailored to fit specific needs regarding the underlying asset, amount, expiration date, and terms of settlement. OTC options are typically

used by institutions for specific hedging needs that cannot be met by standardized exchange-traded options.

Participants in the Options Market

The options market comprises various participants, each with their unique roles and objectives:

- **Retail Investors**: Individual traders and investors who use options for speculation, income generation, or hedging.
- **Institutional Investors**: Entities such as mutual funds, pension funds, and insurance companies that trade options in large volumes, often for hedging purposes.
- **Market Makers**: Firms or individuals who provide liquidity to the market by being ready to buy and sell options at publicly quoted prices. They profit from the bid-ask spread and play a crucial role in facilitating smooth market operations.
- **Clearinghouses**: Organizations associated with exchanges that handle the settlement of traded options, ensuring the terms of contracts are honored. They act as the counterparty to both sides of an options trade, mitigating counterparty risk.

Trading Mechanisms

Options trading involves several key processes:

- **Order Placement**: Traders place orders to buy or sell options through a brokerage platform. Orders can be market orders, which execute at the current market price, or limit orders, which set a specific price at which the trader is willing to buy or sell.

- **Matching and Execution**: Once an order is placed, it is matched with a corresponding order on the exchange. This process can be automated through electronic trading systems that connect buyers and sellers.
- **Clearing and Settlement**: After a trade is executed, the clearinghouse steps in to finalize the transaction, ensuring the transfer of the option from the seller to the buyer and the premium payment from the buyer to the seller.

Option Pricing and Valuation

The value of an option is influenced by several factors, including the price of the underlying asset, the strike price, the time until expiration, volatility, and interest rates. Two main components make up an option's price:

- **Intrinsic Value**: The inherent value of an option if it were exercised immediately. For call options, this is the amount by which the underlying asset's price exceeds the strike price. For put options, it's the amount by which the strike price exceeds the underlying asset's price.
- **Time Value**: The additional value attributed to the possibility that the underlying asset's price might move in a favorable direction before the option expires. Time value decreases as the expiration date approaches, a phenomenon known as time decay.

Conclusion

The options market offers a versatile platform for traders to leverage financial opportunities, hedge against risks, and tailor their investment strategies. Understanding its structure, participants, and mechanisms is fundamental to navigating the market effectively. As traders become more acquainted with the workings of the options market, they can better exploit its potential to achieve their financial goals.

Chapter 2: Setting the Stage for Successful Trading

Before diving into the intricacies of options trading strategies and executions, it's essential to establish a solid foundation. This chapter will guide you through the preliminary steps necessary for successful trading, from selecting the right trading platform to understanding the regulatory environment and developing a disciplined trader's mindset. By setting the stage correctly, you can enhance your trading efficiency, make informed decisions, and manage risks more effectively.

2.1 Choosing the Right Trading Platform

The choice of trading platform can significantly impact your trading experience and success. A suitable platform should offer not just ease of use and reliability but also access to comprehensive market data, analytical tools, and educational resources. We'll discuss what features to look for in a trading platform, how to compare different platforms, and the importance of testing platforms through demo accounts before committing to one.

2.2 Establishing Your Trading Account

Setting up a trading account is more than just filling out an application and funding it. This section will cover the different types of trading accounts available, how to choose the right one for your trading style and objectives, and the importance of understanding the terms and conditions, especially regarding options trading. We'll also touch on the significance of asset allocation and diversification right from the start.

2.3 Understanding the Regulatory Environment

Navigating the regulatory landscape is crucial for every trader. Compliance with rules and regulations ensures your trading activities remain legitimate and protected. This section will provide an overview of the key regulatory bodies, such as the Securities and Exchange Commission (SEC) and the Financial Industry Regulatory Authority (FINRA), and discuss their roles in maintaining fair and orderly markets. We'll also cover essential regulations that affect options trading, including margin requirements and trading restrictions.

2.4 The Importance of a Trading Plan

A well-thought-out trading plan is your roadmap to success in the options market. It should outline your trading goals, risk tolerance, strategies, and criteria for entering and exiting trades. This section will guide you through the process of developing a comprehensive trading plan, emphasizing the need for discipline and consistency in following it.

2.5 Risk Management Fundamentals

Effective risk management is the cornerstone of successful trading. In this section, we'll explore various risk management techniques, including setting stop-loss orders, position sizing, and diversifying your portfolio. Understanding and applying these principles can help you protect your capital and navigate through volatile markets more confidently.

2.6 Continuous Education and Staying Informed

The financial markets are constantly evolving, with new strategies, regulations, and technologies emerging regularly.

Staying informed and continually educating yourself is vital for maintaining and enhancing your trading edge. This section will highlight the importance of ongoing education, reliable sources for market news and analysis, and the benefits of networking with other traders for knowledge sharing and support.

Conclusion

Setting the stage for successful trading involves much more than learning about options strategies. It requires careful preparation, from choosing the right platform and setting up your trading account to understanding regulations and developing a solid trading plan. By addressing these foundational aspects, you equip yourself with the tools and mindset necessary for navigating the options market effectively and positioning yourself for long-term success. As we move forward, keep these principles in mind as they will serve as the bedrock upon which your trading journey is built.

2.1 Essential Trading Tools and Platforms

In the dynamic world of options trading, having access to the right tools and platforms is not just a convenience; it's a necessity. The choice of trading platform and the tools it offers can significantly influence your trading decisions, efficiency, and ultimately, your success in the market. This section delves into the essential features to look for in trading platforms, the variety of tools that can enhance your trading, and tips for selecting the platform that best suits your trading style and goals.

Choosing the Right Trading Platform

A trading platform is your gateway to the markets. It's where you'll spend a significant amount of time analyzing trends, executing trades, and managing your portfolio. Here are key features to consider when selecting a trading platform:

- **User Interface**: The platform should have an intuitive, user-friendly interface that suits your trading style. Ease of navigation and the ability to customize the layout can enhance your trading experience.
- **Reliability and Speed**: In the fast-paced options market, the speed of execution and the reliability of the platform are crucial. Delays or downtime can be costly.
- **Market Data and Analytics**: Access to real-time market data, charting tools, and analytical capabilities is essential for informed decision-making. Look for platforms that offer in-depth analysis tools, including technical indicators and historical data.
- **Educational Resources**: Especially for beginners, platforms that provide educational materials, tutorials, and demo accounts can be invaluable in helping you learn the ropes without risking real money.
- **Costs and Fees**: Understand the fee structure, including commission rates for options trading, any platform fees, and charges for accessing premium features or data.
- **Customer Support**: Efficient, accessible customer support is critical, especially when you encounter issues or have questions about your account.

Essential Trading Tools

Beyond the basic platform features, several tools can significantly enhance your trading effectiveness:

- **Options Pricing Calculators**: These tools help you estimate the fair value of options based on various factors, assisting in strategy selection and trade decision-making.
- **Risk Management Software**: Tools that help you analyze the risk associated with different positions and strategies can be crucial for long-term success.
- **Backtesting Software**: This allows you to test your trading strategies against historical data to assess their viability without risking capital.
- **Economic Calendars**: Keeping track of economic events and announcements can help you anticipate market movements and adjust your strategies accordingly.
- **Mobile Trading Apps**: The ability to trade and monitor your positions on the go can be a significant advantage in today's fast-moving markets.

Tips for Selecting a Trading Platform

- **Assess Your Needs**: Consider your trading style, experience level, and the specific features you need to support your trading activities.
- **Take Advantage of Demos**: Most platforms offer demo or trial versions. Use these to get a feel for the platform's interface and features.

- **Consider Integration**: If you use additional tools or software for analysis or trade execution, ensure they can integrate seamlessly with your chosen platform.
- **Seek Recommendations**: Join trading forums, attend webinars, and network with other traders to get insights into the platforms they use and why.
- **Check Reviews and Ratings**: Look for user reviews and ratings to gauge the platform's reliability, customer service, and overall user satisfaction.

Conclusion

The trading platform and tools you choose play a pivotal role in your trading journey. They not only facilitate the mechanics of trading but also provide the insights and analysis necessary to make informed decisions. Take the time to research and select a platform that aligns with your trading needs, offers the essential tools for options trading, and supports your growth as a trader. Remember, the right platform is an investment in your trading future, one that can significantly impact your effectiveness and efficiency in the options market.

2.2 Setting Up Your Trading Account

Establishing a trading account is a fundamental step in your journey as an options trader. This process involves more than just filling out forms; it's about making informed decisions that align with your trading goals, risk tolerance, and financial situation. This section will guide you through the types of trading accounts, considerations for selecting a brokerage, and key steps in setting up your account.

Types of Trading Accounts

When it comes to options trading, not all accounts are created equal. Understanding the different types of accounts available can help you choose one that best suits your needs:

- **Cash Accounts**: These accounts require you to pay for trades in full at the time of purchase. While cash accounts may limit the types of trades you can execute, they also reduce the risk of margin calls and high leverage.
- **Margin Accounts**: Margin accounts allow you to borrow money from your broker to purchase securities, offering greater purchasing power and the ability to short sell. However, they come with higher risks, including the potential for margin calls if the value of your investments falls below a certain level.
- **Retirement Accounts**: Many brokers offer options trading within Individual Retirement Accounts (IRAs) or other retirement accounts. While trading in a retirement account can offer tax advantages, it may be subject to stricter rules and limitations.

Choosing a Brokerage

Your choice of brokerage can significantly impact your trading experience. Consider the following factors when selecting a brokerage:

- **Commissions and Fees**: Compare the fee structures of different brokerages, including commissions on options trades, account maintenance fees, and any other associated costs.

- **Platform and Tools**: Ensure the brokerage offers a trading platform that meets your needs, with access to the analytical tools, data, and resources you require.
- **Customer Service**: Look for a brokerage with a reputation for excellent customer service and support, especially if you're new to options trading.
- **Regulatory Compliance**: Choose a brokerage that is registered with and regulated by reputable financial authorities, such as the Securities and Exchange Commission (SEC) and the Financial Industry Regulatory Authority (FINRA) in the United States.

Setting Up Your Account

Once you've chosen a brokerage, setting up your trading account involves several key steps:

1. **Application**: Complete the brokerage's account application, which will include personal information, financial details, and your trading experience.
2. **Account Type Selection**: Choose the type of account you wish to open, based on your trading strategy and goals.
3. **Options Trading Approval**: Most brokerages require additional approval for options trading, which may involve filling out a questionnaire about your trading experience and understanding of the risks associated with options.
4. **Funding Your Account**: Once approved, you'll need to fund your account. This can typically be done via bank transfer, check, or wire transfer.

5. **Setting Up Trading Tools**: Customize the brokerage's trading platform to suit your preferences, setting up any necessary charts, watchlists, and analytical tools.
6. **Risk Management Settings**: Establish your risk management parameters, such as setting up default order sizes, stop-loss orders, and other controls to help manage your trading risk.

Conclusion

Setting up your trading account is a crucial step that sets the stage for your trading activities. By carefully selecting the right type of account and brokerage, and taking the time to properly set up and fund your account, you can position yourself for a more effective and efficient trading experience. Remember, the choices you make in this early stage can have a significant impact on your trading journey, so approach this process with the diligence and thoughtfulness it deserves.

2.3 Regulatory Landscape and Compliance

Navigating the regulatory landscape is a critical aspect of options trading. Understanding and adhering to the rules set forth by regulatory bodies ensures that your trading activities are compliant and secure. This section will provide an overview of the key regulatory bodies, the regulations that affect options trading, and the importance of compliance for traders.

Key Regulatory Bodies

In the United States, several organizations regulate the securities and options markets to protect investors and maintain fair, orderly, and efficient markets:

- **Securities and Exchange Commission (SEC)**: The SEC oversees the securities markets and protects investors by enforcing securities laws designed to promote transparency and fairness.
- **Financial Industry Regulatory Authority (FINRA)**: FINRA is a self-regulatory organization that regulates brokerage firms and exchange markets, focusing on investor protection and market integrity.
- **Options Clearing Corporation (OCC)**: The OCC is the world's largest equity derivatives clearing organization, responsible for ensuring the fulfillment of options contracts.
- **Commodity Futures Trading Commission (CFTC)**: For options on commodities and futures, the CFTC plays a similar role to the SEC, overseeing the U.S. derivatives markets.

Key Regulations Affecting Options Trading

Several regulations specifically impact options trading, designed to protect both the trader and the integrity of the markets:

- **Suitability Requirements**: Brokerages are required to ensure that options trading is suitable for a client based on their investment objectives, experience, and financial situation.

- **Margin Requirements**: The Federal Reserve's Regulation T and various exchange rules set forth margin requirements for options trading, which traders must comply with.
- **Pattern Day Trader Rules**: Traders who execute four or more day trades within five business days are considered pattern day traders and are subject to higher minimum equity requirements and potentially other restrictions.
- **Sales Practices and Advertising**: The SEC and FINRA have specific rules governing how financial services can market and advertise options trading, aimed at preventing misleading or fraudulent practices.

Importance of Compliance for Traders

Compliance with regulations is not just a legal obligation but also a best practice that can safeguard your investments:

- **Protecting Your Investments**: Adhering to regulations helps protect your assets from fraud and unauthorized activities.
- **Avoiding Penalties**: Non-compliance can result in fines, restrictions on your trading account, or legal action.
- **Informed Trading**: Understanding regulations encourages informed trading decisions and better risk management.

Staying Informed

Regulations can change, and new rules can be introduced. It's important for traders to stay informed about the regulatory environment:

- **Educational Resources**: Utilize resources provided by regulatory bodies, such as the SEC's and FINRA's websites, for updates and educational materials.
- **Brokerage Communications**: Pay attention to communications from your brokerage, as they often provide updates on regulatory changes that may affect your account.
- **Professional Advice**: Consider consulting with a financial advisor or legal professional specializing in securities law to ensure you fully understand the regulatory requirements relevant to your trading activities.

Conclusion

The regulatory landscape in options trading is designed to protect traders and maintain the integrity of the markets. By understanding and complying with these regulations, you can ensure that your trading activities are both legal and aligned with best practices. Staying informed and seeking professional advice when necessary can help you navigate the complexities of regulations and focus on achieving your trading objectives.

Chapter 3: Developing Your Trading Mindset

Success in options trading isn't solely dependent on knowledge of the markets or mastery of strategies; a significant component is the trader's mindset. A disciplined, resilient, and informed mindset can often be the deciding factor between success and failure in the trading world. This chapter explores the psychological aspects of trading, offering guidance on cultivating the mental resilience and discipline essential for navigating the volatile world of options trading.

3.1 The Psychology of Trading

Trading psychology refers to the emotional and mental states that influence traders' decisions. Understanding and managing these psychological factors can help you make more rational decisions, free from the biases and emotions that often lead to costly mistakes.

- **Emotional Control**: Learn to recognize and control emotions like fear, greed, and hope, which can cloud judgment and lead to impulsive decisions.
- **Cognitive Biases**: Be aware of common cognitive biases that affect traders, such as overconfidence, confirmation bias, and loss aversion, and develop strategies to mitigate their impact.

3.2 Developing Discipline and Patience

Discipline and patience are vital traits for any trader, particularly in the options market where opportunities may unfold over longer time horizons.

- **Adhering to Your Trading Plan**: Discipline is about sticking to your trading plan, even in the face of market volatility or when trades don't go as expected.
- **Patience in Trade Execution and Management**: Cultivate patience by waiting for the right trading opportunities and avoiding the urge to overtrade.

3.3 Handling Losses and Setbacks

Losses are an inevitable part of trading, but how you handle them can significantly affect your overall success.

- **Learning from Losses**: View losses as learning opportunities. Analyze what went wrong and how you can improve in the future.
- **Maintaining Perspective**: Keep individual losses and setbacks in perspective, focusing on long-term goals and overall portfolio performance.

3.4 The Importance of Continuous Learning

The financial markets are constantly evolving, and successful traders are those who commit to lifelong learning.

- **Staying Informed**: Keep abreast of market trends, economic indicators, and new trading strategies.

- **Skill Development**: Regularly review and refine your trading skills, and be open to exploring new techniques and approaches.

3.5 Building a Support Network

Trading can be a solitary activity, but having a support network can provide valuable perspectives and emotional support.

- **Joining Trading Communities**: Engage with online forums, trading groups, and professional associations to share experiences and learn from others.
- **Seeking Professional Guidance**: Consider working with a mentor or coach who can provide guidance, share insights, and help you navigate challenging periods.

3.6 Maintaining Work-Life Balance

Ensuring a healthy balance between trading and other life activities is crucial for sustaining the mental and emotional energy needed for trading.

- **Setting Boundaries**: Allocate specific times for trading and ensure you have time for relaxation, hobbies, and spending time with family and friends.
- **Managing Stress**: Adopt stress management practices such as regular exercise, meditation, or other relaxation techniques to maintain a clear mind.

Conclusion

Developing a robust trading mindset is as critical as mastering technical skills. By cultivating emotional control, discipline, patience, and a commitment to continuous learning, you can significantly enhance your trading performance. Remember, the journey to becoming a successful options trader is not just about the trades you make but also about the mindset with which you approach the market.

3.1 The Psychology of Trading

The realm of trading is not just a test of knowledge and strategy but also a profound psychological journey. The psychology of trading encompasses the mental and emotional aspects that influence decision-making in the markets. This section delves into the critical components of trading psychology, highlighting the importance of emotional control, understanding cognitive biases, and developing a resilient mindset to navigate the often turbulent waters of options trading.

Emotional Control in Trading

Emotions can be a trader's greatest adversary, clouding judgment and leading to impulsive decisions that diverge from well-laid plans. Key emotions to manage include:

- **Fear**: Fear of loss can lead to premature selling or avoiding potentially profitable trades. Conversely, the fear of missing out (FOMO) can prompt ill-timed entries into trades.

- **Greed**: Greed can drive traders to hold onto positions too long in the hope of higher profits, risking significant losses when the market turns.
- **Hope**: Hope can lead traders to hold losing positions too long, waiting for the market to reverse and turn losses into profits, often exacerbating the situation.

Developing emotional control involves recognizing these emotions and mitigating their influence through disciplined adherence to your trading plan and strategies.

Cognitive Biases Affecting Traders

Cognitive biases are systematic patterns of deviation from rationality in judgment, and they can significantly impact trading decisions:

- **Overconfidence Bias**: Overestimating one's knowledge or ability can lead to taking excessive risks.
- **Confirmation Bias**: Seeking information that confirms one's preexisting beliefs or hypotheses can lead to ignoring contradictory evidence.
- **Loss Aversion**: The tendency to prefer avoiding losses over acquiring equivalent gains can lead to holding losing positions too long or selling winning positions too early.

Awareness of these biases is the first step in minimizing their impact, enabling more rational, objective decision-making in trading.

Building a Resilient Trading Mindset

Resilience in trading is about maintaining focus and composure, even during market downturns or personal setbacks. This involves:

- **Acceptance**: Recognizing that losses are part of trading and learning from them without letting emotions take control.
- **Perspective**: Keeping individual trades in perspective regarding your overall trading plan and long-term goals.
- **Flexibility**: Being willing to adapt your strategies in response to changing market conditions while remaining true to your overall trading philosophy.

Stress Management and Mental Health

Stress and mental health play significant roles in trading psychology. Effective stress management techniques, such as regular exercise, meditation, and ensuring a healthy work-life balance, are crucial for maintaining mental clarity and emotional equilibrium.

Conclusion

The psychological aspect of trading is as critical as the technical skills. Mastering trading psychology involves developing emotional control, being aware of and minimizing cognitive biases, building resilience, and managing stress effectively. By fostering a healthy trading mindset, you can enhance your decision-making process, stick to your trading plan more consistently, and ultimately, improve your trading performance. Remember, successful trading isn't just about making the right moves in the market; it's also about mastering the mind that makes those moves.

3.2 Risk Management Fundamentals

In the volatile world of options trading, effective risk management is not just a practice—it's a necessity. The inherent leverage in options can amplify gains, but it can also exacerbate losses, making a well-structured approach to risk management crucial for long-term success. This section explores the foundational principles of risk management in options trading, offering strategies to preserve capital and maintain a healthy trading portfolio.

Understanding Risk in Options Trading

Before delving into risk management strategies, it's essential to understand the unique risks associated with options trading:

- **Leverage Risk**: The leveraged nature of options means small market movements can lead to significant changes in the value of an options position.
- **Time Decay**: Options are "wasting assets" due to their limited life span, which can erode the value of an option over time, especially if the market doesn't move as anticipated.
- **Volatility Risk**: Options prices are sensitive to changes in the volatility of the underlying asset, which can impact the value of an option independently of the price movement of the underlying asset.

Key Risk Management Strategies

Effective risk management involves a combination of strategies designed to mitigate the risks associated with options trading:

- **Position Sizing**: Determine the appropriate size for each trade based on a percentage of your total trading capital to avoid overexposure to a single trade.
- **Diversification**: Spread your investments across various assets, markets, and strategies to reduce the impact of a poor performing position on your overall portfolio.
- **Use of Stop-Loss Orders**: Implement stop-loss orders to automatically close out positions at a predetermined price level, limiting potential losses.
- **Hedging**: Employ hedging strategies, such as protective puts or covered calls, to offset potential losses in your portfolio.

Balancing Risk and Reward

An integral part of risk management is balancing the potential risk with the expected reward of a trade:

- **Risk/Reward Ratio**: Evaluate the potential downside of a trade relative to its upside, aiming for trades where the potential reward justifies the risk taken.
- **Profit Targets and Loss Limits**: Set clear profit targets and loss limits for each trade to ensure disciplined decision-making and to prevent emotional trading.

The Importance of a Trading Plan

A comprehensive trading plan is vital for effective risk management, detailing your trading strategy, entry and exit criteria, risk tolerance, and money management rules. Adherence to a well-thought-out trading plan can help maintain discipline and consistency in your trading approach.

Continuous Monitoring and Review

Risk management is an ongoing process that requires continuous monitoring and review of your trading activities:

- **Regular Portfolio Review**: Periodically review your portfolio to assess performance, ensure alignment with your risk tolerance, and make adjustments as necessary.
- **Performance Analysis**: Analyze both successful and unsuccessful trades to understand the risks encountered and to refine your risk management strategies.

Conclusion

Risk management is the cornerstone of sustainable trading practices. By understanding the unique risks associated with options trading and implementing sound risk management strategies, you can protect your capital, limit losses, and position yourself for long-term success in the options market. Remember, the goal of risk management is not to eliminate risk but to manage it intelligently, enabling you to navigate the markets with confidence.

3.3 Building Discipline and Patience in Trading

In the high-stakes environment of options trading, discipline and patience are not just virtues—they are essential components for success. The ability to adhere to a well-defined trading plan and wait for the right opportunities can differentiate between thriving in the market and facing unnecessary losses. This section will explore strategies to cultivate these crucial traits, helping you to make more informed decisions and enhance your overall trading performance.

The Role of Discipline in Trading

Discipline in trading means sticking to your trading plan, rules, and strategies without letting emotions drive your decisions. It involves:

- **Predefined Rules**: Establishing clear criteria for entering and exiting trades, including profit targets and stop-loss levels, and adhering to these rules consistently.
- **Emotional Control**: Maintaining composure and resisting the urge to make impulsive decisions based on short-term market movements or emotional reactions.
- **Routine and Process**: Developing and following a daily trading routine that includes market analysis, trade review, and continuous learning.

Cultivating Patience in Trading

Patience in trading is the ability to wait for the right trading conditions and setups, rather than acting on every perceived opportunity. It includes:

- **Selective Trading**: Waiting for trade setups that fully meet your criteria, rather than overtrading or chasing the market.
- **Long-Term Perspective**: Focusing on long-term goals and overall portfolio performance, rather than getting swayed by short-term fluctuations.
- **Waiting Out Positions**: Allowing winning trades to reach their full potential, in accordance with your trading plan, rather than exiting too early due to impatience.

Strategies to Build Discipline and Patience

Building discipline and patience requires intentional practice and strategies:

- **Set Realistic Goals**: Establish achievable trading goals that align with your experience level and trading strategy, helping to keep expectations in check and foster patience.
- **Journaling**: Maintain a trading journal to record your trades, emotional state, and decision-making process. Reviewing your journal can provide insights into impulsive decisions and help reinforce discipline.
- **Mindfulness and Stress Reduction**: Practices such as meditation, exercise, or other stress-reduction

techniques can improve emotional regulation, aiding in the development of patience and discipline.

- **Simulation and Backtesting**: Use simulation trading and backtesting strategies to practice discipline and patience in a risk-free environment.
- **Limiting Exposure**: Set limits on your trading activity, such as the number of trades per day or maximum allowable losses, to enforce discipline.
- **Continuous Education**: Engage in continuous learning to deepen your understanding of the markets and your trading strategy, reinforcing the rationale behind your disciplined approach.

The Importance of Consistency

Consistency in applying discipline and patience is key to their effectiveness. It involves:

- **Regular Review**: Regularly review your trading plan, goals, and performance to ensure consistency in your approach.
- **Accountability**: Consider seeking a trading mentor or joining a trading community to provide accountability and encouragement to remain disciplined and patient.

Conclusion

Discipline and patience are foundational to successful trading, enabling you to navigate the markets with a strategic, measured approach. By implementing the strategies outlined above, you can cultivate these traits, leading to more deliberate decision-making and improved trading outcomes. Remember, trading is not just about the strategies you employ but also about the mindset with which you approach the market.

Chapter 4: Crafting Your Options Trading Strategy

Developing a coherent and effective options trading strategy is pivotal for navigating the complexities of the market and achieving long-term success. This chapter delves into the process of building a trading strategy that aligns with your financial goals, risk tolerance, and market outlook. We'll explore various strategic considerations, from basic buy and hold approaches to more advanced strategies, and discuss how to tailor these strategies to fit your trading profile.

4.1 Understanding Your Trading Profile

Before crafting a strategy, it's essential to assess your trading profile, which includes your financial goals, risk tolerance, market experience, and time commitment. This self-assessment will guide your strategy selection, ensuring it aligns with your personal and financial objectives.

- **Financial Goals**: Are you seeking capital growth, income generation, or portfolio hedging?
- **Risk Tolerance**: How much capital are you willing to risk, and what level of market volatility can you withstand?
- **Market Experience**: Do you have a deep understanding of options and the underlying markets, or are you still learning?
- **Time Commitment**: How much time can you dedicate to market research, trading, and strategy adjustment?

4.2 Fundamental Options Trading Strategies

Start with the fundamentals. Understanding basic options strategies is crucial, as they form the building blocks for more complex trades:

- **Buying Calls and Puts**: Simple strategies for speculative bets on directional market movements.
- **Covered Calls**: Generating income on existing stock positions by selling call options against them.
- **Protective Puts**: Insuring your stock holdings against significant declines by purchasing put options.

4.3 Advanced Options Strategies

Once you're comfortable with the basics, consider exploring advanced strategies that can offer more nuanced market positions and risk management capabilities:

- **Spreads**: Utilizing combinations of options purchases and sales to cap potential losses while providing profit opportunities, such as bull spreads, bear spreads, and calendar spreads.
- **Straddles and Strangles**: Strategies that allow you to profit from significant market moves in either direction, useful in highly volatile market conditions.
- **Butterflies and Condors**: More complex strategies designed to profit from specific ranges in the underlying market, with limited risk.

4.4 Strategy Selection and Customization

Selecting the right strategy involves matching your trading profile with the appropriate strategy's risk/reward profile. Considerations include:

- **Market Outlook**: Is your view on the underlying market bullish, bearish, or neutral? Does it anticipate high volatility or relatively stable conditions?
- **Capital Allocation**: How much of your trading capital are you willing to allocate to a particular strategy?
- **Adjustment and Exit Plans**: Define clear criteria for adjusting or exiting a position if the market moves against you or your outlook changes.

4.5 Backtesting and Paper Trading

Before implementing a new strategy with real capital, test it thoroughly through backtesting against historical data and paper trading in real-time market conditions. This testing can help refine the strategy, understand its potential pitfalls, and adjust for risk management.

4.6 Continuous Strategy Evaluation

Market conditions change, and even a well-crafted strategy may need adjustments over time. Regularly review your strategy's performance, market alignment, and alignment with your trading goals. Be prepared to modify your approach as your experience grows and market conditions evolve.

Conclusion

Crafting an effective options trading strategy requires a deep understanding of your trading profile, a solid grasp of fundamental and advanced options strategies, and a commitment to continuous learning and adaptation. By carefully selecting and tailoring strategies to fit your goals and risk tolerance, and by rigorously testing and evaluating your approach, you can build a robust trading plan that navigates market complexities and works towards achieving your financial objectives. Remember, the key to successful options trading lies not just in the strategies you choose but in how well they align with your overall trading philosophy and goals.

4.1 Analyzing Market Trends

Analyzing market trends is a crucial step in crafting your options trading strategy. Understanding the direction and strength of market movements can help you make informed decisions about which options strategies to employ and when to execute them. This section explores the fundamental and technical analysis tools you can use to gauge market trends and how to apply this analysis to your options trading approach.

Understanding Market Trends

Market trends can be broadly classified into three categories: uptrends, downtrends, and sideways trends. Recognizing these trends is essential for selecting the appropriate options strategy:

- **Uptrends** are characterized by higher highs and higher lows, indicating a bullish market sentiment.
- **Downtrends** are marked by lower highs and lower lows, signaling bearish market conditions.
- **Sideways trends** occur when the market is range-bound, with no clear direction in prices.

Fundamental Analysis

Fundamental analysis involves evaluating economic, financial, and other qualitative and quantitative factors to determine an asset's intrinsic value and potential for future growth. For options traders, fundamental analysis can provide context for long-term trends and potential market shifts:

- **Economic Indicators**: Gross Domestic Product (GDP), employment rates, inflation, and consumer confidence can provide insights into the overall health of the economy and potential market directions.
- **Earnings Reports**: Company earnings, revenue, and growth projections can influence stock prices and, consequently, options valuations.
- **Industry Trends**: Sector-specific developments, regulatory changes, and competitive dynamics can impact companies' performance within an industry, affecting related options.

Technical Analysis

Technical analysis focuses on analyzing historical market data, primarily price and volume, to forecast future price movements. This analysis is particularly useful for options traders looking to identify entry and exit points:

- **Trend Lines**: Drawing lines connecting highs or lows to identify the direction of the market trend.
- **Support and Resistance Levels**: Identifying price levels at which a stock historically fails to move higher (resistance) or lower (support), which can indicate potential trend reversals or continuations.
- **Moving Averages**: Utilizing moving averages to smooth out price data and identify the direction of the trend. Crossovers of short-term and long-term moving averages can signal potential trend changes.
- **Momentum Indicators**: Tools like the Relative Strength Index (RSI) or MACD (Moving Average Convergence Divergence) help gauge the strength of a trend and potential reversal points.

Applying Trend Analysis to Options Trading

Understanding market trends allows options traders to choose strategies that align with the current market environment:

- **In Uptrends**: Consider bullish strategies such as buying calls, bull spreads, or writing put options.
- **In Downtrends**: Bearish strategies like buying puts, bear spreads, or writing call options may be appropriate.
- **In Sideways Trends**: Neutral strategies, such as iron condors or butterflies, can capitalize on range-bound markets.

The Importance of Context

While trend analysis is a powerful tool, it's essential to consider it within the broader market context. Economic news, geopolitical events, and market sentiment can all influence market trends and should be factored into your analysis and decision-making process.

Conclusion

Analyzing market trends is a foundational skill for options traders, providing insights that inform strategy selection and execution. By combining fundamental and technical analysis, you can develop a nuanced understanding of market dynamics, helping you to navigate the complexities of options trading with greater confidence and precision. Remember, the goal is not to predict the market with certainty but to identify probabilities and manage risks accordingly.

4.2 Technical Analysis Basics

Technical analysis is a critical tool for options traders, providing insights into future market movements based on past and current price action and volume data. This methodology assumes that all known information is already reflected in prices, and that prices move in trends. Understanding the basics of technical analysis can help you identify potential entry and exit points, forecast market direction, and select appropriate options strategies. This section covers the foundational elements of technical analysis and their application in options trading.

Chart Types

The first step in technical analysis is to understand the different types of charts used to visualize price movements:

- **Line Charts**: The simplest form, showing the closing prices of an asset over time, which can help identify overall trends.
- **Bar Charts**: Provide more information than line charts, including opening, high, low, and closing prices (OHLC) for each period, offering a clearer view of price movements and volatility.
- **Candlestick Charts**: Similar to bar charts but use colored "candles" to represent price movements. Green (or white) candles indicate price increases, while red (or black) candles signify price decreases, offering insights into market sentiment and potential reversals.

Trend Analysis

Identifying trends is a cornerstone of technical analysis, as "the trend is your friend":

- **Uptrends**: Characterized by a series of higher highs and higher lows. In an uptrend, traders might look for opportunities to buy calls or sell puts.
- **Downtrends**: Defined by lower highs and lower lows. In a downtrend, traders may consider buying puts or selling calls.
- **Sideways Trends**: When the market is moving within a range without a clear direction. Options strategies like iron condors or straddles might be suitable in these conditions.

Support and Resistance

Support and resistance levels are price points where the market tends to reverse or pause, due to a concentration of demand (support) or supply (resistance):

- **Support**: A level where buying interest is significantly strong and surpasses selling pressure, preventing the price from falling further.
- **Resistance**: A level where selling interest overcomes buying pressure, stopping the price from rising higher.

Understanding these levels can help traders make strategic decisions about entry and exit points and set stop-loss orders.

Technical Indicators and Oscillators

Technical indicators are mathematical calculations based on price, volume, or open interest of a security, used to forecast future price movements:

- **Moving Averages**: Indicators that smooth out price data to identify the trend direction. The crossover of short-term and long-term moving averages can signal potential market reversals.
- **Momentum Indicators**: Such as the Relative Strength Index (RSI) and MACD, measure the speed of price movements, helping to identify overbought or oversold conditions.

Chart Patterns

Chart patterns are formations within price charts that indicate what prices might do next, based on historical performance:

- **Continuation Patterns**: Such as triangles, flags, and pennants, suggest that the prevailing trend will continue.
- **Reversal Patterns**: Like head and shoulders, double tops/bottoms, and cup and handle, indicate that the current trend may reverse.

Volume Analysis

Volume, the number of shares or contracts traded in a security or market, is a significant factor in technical analysis, as it can confirm trends and signal the strength of a price move.

Putting It All Together

Incorporating technical analysis into your options trading strategy involves combining these elements to make informed decisions. For example, identifying a bullish trend with strong volume and a momentum indicator that signals an overbought condition might suggest a potential reversal, influencing your options strategy selection.

Conclusion

Technical analysis is a powerful tool in the options trader's toolkit, offering a data-driven basis for decision-making. By understanding and applying its principles, you can enhance your ability to predict market movements, select appropriate trading strategies, and manage risk more effectively. Remember, while technical analysis can provide valuable insights, it's most effective when used in conjunction with a solid understanding of options fundamentals and market conditions.

4.3 Fundamental Analysis in Options Trading

While technical analysis focuses on price movements and trends, fundamental analysis delves into the economic and financial factors that underpin a company's value and potential for growth. For options traders, especially those with a longer-term outlook or those trading options on indexes and ETFs, incorporating fundamental analysis can provide a broader context for market movements and inform strategy selection. This section explores how fundamental analysis can be applied in options trading, from assessing company health to understanding macroeconomic indicators.

Company Health and Earnings

At the core of fundamental analysis for individual stocks is an assessment of the company's financial health and performance:

- **Earnings Reports**: Quarterly and annual earnings reports are critical for evaluating a company's profitability and growth potential. Significant earnings surprises, either positive or negative, can lead to substantial price movements, impacting options pricing and strategy selection.
- **Balance Sheet Analysis**: Reviewing a company's assets, liabilities, and shareholder equity provides insights into its financial stability and ability to sustain operations and growth.
- **Cash Flow Statements**: Understanding how a company generates and uses cash can highlight its operational efficiency and financial health, influencing its stock's long-term trajectory.

Industry and Sector Analysis

Options traders can benefit from analyzing the industry and sector in which a company operates:

- **Industry Trends**: Emerging or declining trends within an industry can impact companies differently, affecting their stock prices and, consequently, options valuations.
- **Competitive Positioning**: A company's position within its industry, its competitive advantages, and market share can provide clues about its potential for future success.

Macroeconomic Factors

Options trading, particularly on broader indexes or ETFs, can be influenced by macroeconomic factors:

- **Economic Indicators**: GDP growth rates, unemployment figures, inflation data, and consumer confidence indices can signal the overall health of the economy, influencing market sentiment and direction.
- **Monetary Policy**: Central bank policies, including interest rates and quantitative easing measures, can significantly impact market conditions, affecting the valuation of options across different sectors.
- **Geopolitical Events**: Events such as elections, trade negotiations, and geopolitical tensions can create market volatility, presenting both risks and opportunities for options traders.

Applying Fundamental Analysis in Options Trading

Integrating fundamental analysis into your options trading strategy involves:

- **Long-Term Positioning**: Using fundamental analysis to identify companies or sectors with strong growth potential or undervaluation for long-term options plays, such as LEAPS (Long-term Equity Anticipation Securities).
- **Event-Driven Strategies**: Capitalizing on anticipated earnings releases, product launches, or regulatory decisions by employing strategies that benefit from increased volatility, such as straddles or strangles.
- **Macro-Themed Strategies**: Utilizing options on indexes, ETFs, or sectors that are poised to benefit from macroeconomic trends or shifts in monetary policy.

Conclusion

Fundamental analysis provides a deep dive into the economic, financial, and industry-specific factors that drive market movements and company valuations. For options traders, integrating fundamental insights can enhance strategy selection, particularly for those looking at longer-term positions or trading based on broader market themes. While fundamental analysis may require more time and effort than technical analysis, its contribution to a well-rounded trading approach can be invaluable, offering a comprehensive view of the market landscape and underlying trends.

4.4 Crafting Your First Trading Plan

A well-defined trading plan is essential for navigating the complexities of options trading. It serves as a roadmap, guiding your decisions and helping you maintain discipline, especially in volatile markets. Crafting your first trading plan involves outlining your trading goals, strategies, risk management rules, and criteria for evaluating performance. This section will walk you through the steps to create a comprehensive trading plan tailored to your objectives and risk tolerance.

Define Your Trading Objectives

Start by clearly defining what you want to achieve through options trading. Objectives can vary from capital appreciation and income generation to hedging existing positions. Be specific about your financial goals and the timeframe you have in mind to achieve them.

Assess Your Risk Tolerance

Understanding your risk tolerance is crucial for developing a trading plan that aligns with your comfort level. Consider factors such as your financial situation, investment experience, and emotional response to potential losses. Define the maximum percentage of your portfolio you are willing to risk on a single trade and the overall level of risk you're comfortable with for your options trading activities.

Select Your Trading Strategies

Based on your objectives and risk tolerance, choose the options trading strategies that best suit your goals. For beginners, it might be wise to start with more straightforward strategies, such as buying calls or puts and writing covered calls. As you gain experience, you can gradually explore more complex strategies like spreads, straddles, and condors.

Establish Entry and Exit Criteria

Clearly define the conditions under which you will enter and exit trades. Entry criteria might include specific technical indicators, fundamental analysis insights, or market conditions that signal a trading opportunity. Similarly, establish exit criteria to lock in profits or cut losses, such as reaching a desired profit target, hitting a stop-loss level, or a significant change in market conditions.

Set Rules for Money Management

Money management rules are a critical component of your trading plan, helping you preserve capital and manage risk. Decide on the amount of capital you will allocate to each trade and how you will adjust position sizes based on your trading account's overall performance. Consider setting a daily or weekly loss limit to prevent emotional decision-making in challenging market conditions.

Develop a Routine for Market Analysis

Consistency in analyzing the market is key to identifying trading opportunities. Outline a routine for reviewing market conditions, monitoring economic news, and analyzing charts. Determine which technical indicators and fundamental analysis tools you will rely on and how often you will review your watchlist of potential trades.

Plan for Record-Keeping and Review

Maintaining a trading journal is essential for evaluating your performance and refining your trading plan. Record details of each trade, including the rationale for entering and exiting, the outcome, and any lessons learned. Regularly review your trading journal to identify patterns in your trading, assess the effectiveness of your strategies, and make adjustments to your plan as necessary.

Conclusion

Your first trading plan is a foundational document that will evolve as you gain experience and insights into your trading preferences and the market's nuances. It should be comprehensive yet flexible, allowing for adjustments as you learn from your trading experiences. By adhering to your trading plan, you can approach the market with confidence, make informed decisions, and navigate the ups and downs of options trading with discipline and clarity. Remember, the most successful traders are those who plan their trades and trade their plan.

Chapter 5: Advanced Options Trading Strategies

After mastering the basics of options trading and gaining experience with fundamental strategies, you may be ready to explore more advanced techniques. These strategies can offer greater flexibility, more sophisticated risk management options, and the potential for significant returns. However, they also come with increased complexity and risk. This chapter delves into several advanced options trading strategies, outlining their construction, ideal market conditions, and potential risks and rewards.

5.1 Spreads

Spreads involve simultaneously buying and selling options of the same type (either calls or puts) with different strike prices and/or expiration dates. They are used to limit potential losses while still providing an opportunity for profit.

- **Vertical Spreads**: Combine options with the same expiration date but different strike prices. Bull call spreads and bear put spreads are examples that bet on directional movements while limiting risk.
- **Horizontal (Calendar) Spreads**: Involve options of the same strike price but different expiration dates, capitalizing on differences in time decay.
- **Diagonal Spreads**: A combination of vertical and horizontal spreads, using options with different strike prices and expiration dates, to benefit from both price movements and time decay.

5.2 Straddles and Strangles

These strategies are ideal for situations where significant price movement is expected but the direction is uncertain.

- **Straddles**: Involve buying a call and a put option with the same strike price and expiration date. This strategy profits if the underlying asset moves significantly in either direction.
- **Strangles**: Similar to straddles but use out-of-the-money (OTM) options, reducing the upfront cost at the expense of needing a larger price move to profit.

5.3 Butterfly Spreads

Butterfly spreads involve combining multiple options positions to create a payoff profile resembling a butterfly's wings. They are typically used to profit from a stock trading in a narrow range.

- **Long Butterfly Spread**: Involves buying one in-the-money (ITM) option, selling two at-the-money (ATM) options, and buying one out-of-the-money (OTM) option. It offers limited risk and is ideal for a neutral market outlook.

5.4 Iron Condors

An iron condor is a more complex strategy that involves four different options to profit from a stock trading within a certain range without significant price movement.

- **Construction**: Sell one OTM put, buy one put with a lower strike price, sell one OTM call, and buy one call with a higher strike price. All options have the same expiration date.

- **Market Outlook**: Ideal for a neutral market where significant price movement is not anticipated.

5.5 Managing Risk with Advanced Strategies

While advanced options strategies can offer appealing risk-reward profiles, they require thorough understanding and careful management:

- **Understand the Max Loss and Profit**: Before entering any advanced trade, know the maximum potential loss and profit, and ensure they align with your risk tolerance.
- **Monitor and Adjust**: These strategies often require active management. Be prepared to adjust your positions in response to market movements.
- **Costs and Commissions**: Multiple transactions mean higher trading costs, which can eat into potential profits. Consider this in your planning.

Conclusion

Advanced options trading strategies offer seasoned traders sophisticated tools to express their market views, manage risk, and seek profits. However, the complexity and risk associated with these strategies necessitate a deep understanding of options mechanics and active trade management. Always ensure that advanced strategies align with your overall trading goals, risk tolerance, and market outlook before implementation. As you grow more comfortable with these strategies, they can become a valuable part of your trading arsenal, offering nuanced approaches to the options market.

5.1 Spreads: Bull and Bear

Spreads are versatile options strategies that traders employ to take advantage of various market conditions while managing risk. Among the most common are bull spreads and bear spreads, designed to profit from upward or downward market movements, respectively. This section will delve into the mechanics, ideal market conditions, and potential risks and rewards of these spread strategies.

Bull Spreads

Bull spreads are used when a trader expects a moderate rise in the price of the underlying asset. This strategy involves simultaneously buying and selling call options with the same expiration date but different strike prices.

- **Long Call Bull Spread**: Buy a call option at a lower strike price (more expensive, in-the-money or at-the-money) and sell a call option at a higher strike price (less expensive, out-of-the-money). The maximum profit is capped at the difference between the two strike prices, minus the net premium paid. The maximum loss is limited to the net premium paid for the spread.
- **Ideal Market Conditions**: Best used when expecting a moderate increase in the underlying asset's price. The strategy benefits from upward movements but has limited risk if the market moves against the trader.

Bear Spreads

Bear spreads are the opposite of bull spreads and are utilized when a trader anticipates a moderate decline in the price of the underlying asset. This strategy typically involves buying and selling put options.

- **Long Put Bear Spread**: Buy a put option at a higher strike price (more expensive, in-the-money or at-the-money) and sell a put option at a lower strike price (less expensive, out-of-the-money). The maximum profit is capped at the difference between the two strike prices, minus the net premium paid, and occurs if the price of the underlying asset is at or below the lower strike price at expiration. The maximum loss is limited to the net premium paid.
- **Ideal Market Conditions**: Suited for situations where a moderate decline in the underlying asset's price is expected. It offers a defined risk profile if the market direction is misjudged.

Managing Risks with Spreads

While bull and bear spreads limit potential losses to the net premium paid, it's crucial to manage these positions actively:

- **Break-Even Point**: Understand where the break-even point lies for your spread strategy. For bull spreads, it's the lower strike price plus the net premium paid. For bear spreads, it's the higher strike price minus the net premium paid.
- **Volatility Considerations**: While spreads can benefit from directional moves, implied volatility changes can

impact the value of your spread. A rise in volatility typically benefits long positions but may be detrimental when you're short an option.

- **Time Decay**: Time decay (theta) plays a role, especially as the options approach expiration. The value of your positions may erode if the expected move in the underlying asset does not occur quickly enough.

Conclusion

Bull and bear spreads offer traders a way to express a directional view on the market with limited risk. By carefully selecting strike prices and managing positions in response to market movements, traders can use these strategies to pursue moderate profits in bullish or bearish conditions while keeping potential losses in check. As with all options strategies, a thorough understanding of the underlying mechanics and market conditions is essential for successful implementation.

5.2 The Iron Condor and Straddle Strategies

The iron condor and straddle are two advanced options trading strategies that cater to different market outlooks. The iron condor is preferred in a market with low volatility and minimal price movement, while the straddle strategy is ideal for markets expected to experience significant volatility in either direction. This section will explore the construction, ideal conditions, and potential risks and rewards associated with these strategies.

Iron Condor Strategy

An iron condor involves combining four options contracts to capitalize on a stock trading within a specific range without significant price movement. It's constructed by selling an out-of-the-money (OTM) call, buying a further OTM call, selling an OTM put, and buying a further OTM put, all with the same expiration date.

- **Construction**: For example, sell a $105 call, buy a $110 call, sell a $95 put, and buy a $90 put on the same stock with the same expiration date. This creates a profit zone between the sold call and put strike prices.
- **Ideal Market Conditions**: Best suited for neutral markets where significant price movement is not anticipated. The strategy profits from time decay and low volatility.
- **Risk/Reward**: The maximum profit is limited to the net premium received from establishing the positions. The maximum loss is the difference between the strike prices of the bought and sold options, minus the net premium received.

Straddle Strategy

A straddle involves buying a call and a put option with the same strike price and expiration date. This non-directional strategy profits from significant price movements in either direction.

- **Construction**: For example, buy a $100 call and a $100 put on the same stock with the same expiration date.

This position benefits from significant moves up or down in the underlying stock's price.

- **Ideal Market Conditions**: Suitable in highly volatile markets or ahead of major news events or earnings announcements, where substantial price swings are expected.
- **Risk/Reward**: The potential profit is unlimited if the stock makes a significant move in either direction. The maximum loss is limited to the total premium paid for both the call and the put options.

Managing Risks with Iron Condors and Straddles

Both strategies require careful risk management due to their complex nature:

- **Iron Condor**: The key to managing risk is closely monitoring the underlying asset's price as it approaches the sold strike prices. Adjustments or closing the position may be necessary to mitigate losses.
- **Straddle**: Due to the high cost of purchasing both a call and a put, it's crucial to enter a straddle when option premiums are relatively low, and a significant price movement is anticipated to justify the initial investment.

Conclusion

The iron condor and straddle strategies offer options traders sophisticated tools for navigating different market conditions. The iron condor is well-suited for range-bound markets with low volatility, providing a way to generate income with defined risk. The straddle strategy, on the other hand, is ideal for volatile markets, allowing traders to profit from significant price movements without predicting the direction. Both strategies require a thorough understanding of options mechanics, vigilant risk management, and an ability to make timely adjustments based on market movements.

5.3 Leveraging Options for Portfolio Management

Options are not only powerful tools for speculation and income generation but also for enhancing portfolio management. By integrating options strategies into your portfolio, you can achieve various objectives such as hedging against market downturns, enhancing portfolio yield, and managing risk more effectively. This section explores how options can be leveraged for portfolio management, highlighting strategies for hedging, income generation, and diversification.

Hedging with Options

One of the primary uses of options in portfolio management is hedging, which involves taking positions to offset potential losses in your portfolio.

- **Protective Puts**: Buying put options on stocks or ETFs you own can act as insurance against a significant drop in value. If the stock price falls below the put's strike price, the put option increases in value, offsetting the stock's loss.
- **Collars**: This strategy involves holding the underlying asset, buying a protective put, and selling a call option to offset the put's cost. The call sale caps the upside

potential but provides downside protection with minimal or no net cost.

Income Generation

Options can also be used to generate income on existing portfolio holdings, enhancing overall returns.

- **Covered Calls**: By selling call options on stocks you own, you can earn premium income. This strategy is ideal for stocks with little expected short-term upside, as the call sale provides income but obligates you to sell the stock if it exceeds the strike price.
- **Cash-Secured Puts**: Selling put options on stocks you're willing to own can generate income through premiums. If the stock price falls below the strike price, you may be obligated to buy the stock at that price, potentially at a discount to current levels.

Portfolio Diversification

Options can introduce new strategies and exposures without significant capital outlay, aiding in portfolio diversification.

- **Synthetic Positions**: Options can mimic the payoff profiles of other assets. For example, a synthetic long stock position involves buying a call and selling a put with the same strike price and expiration, replicating stock ownership without buying the actual stock.
- **Access to Different Markets**: Options on different assets, such as commodities, currencies, and indexes, can provide exposure to markets outside of traditional equities, broadening diversification.

Managing Risks

While options can enhance portfolio management, it's crucial to understand and manage the associated risks.

- **Understand the Strategies**: Each options strategy comes with its own risk-reward profile. Ensure you fully understand the potential outcomes before implementation.
- **Monitor and Adjust**: Options positions may require adjustments based on market movements or changes in your investment outlook.
- **Allocation Limits**: Consider setting limits on how much of your portfolio is exposed to options to avoid overconcentration in complex strategies.

Conclusion

Leveraging options for portfolio management can offer significant benefits, from hedging against downside risk to generating additional income and enhancing diversification. However, the complexity and inherent risks of options trading necessitate a thorough understanding of the strategies involved and disciplined risk management. By carefully integrating options into your portfolio management approach, you can tap into their potential to achieve a more robust, flexible, and potentially profitable investment portfolio.

Chapter 6: Common Pitfalls and How to Avoid Them

Options trading, with its potential for high returns, also comes with unique challenges and pitfalls that can ensnare even the most experienced traders. Awareness of these common mistakes and implementing strategies to avoid them can significantly enhance your trading success and longevity in the market. This chapter outlines some of the frequent missteps in options trading and provides guidance on how to navigate around them.

6.1 Overleveraging

The leverage provided by options can amplify profits but also losses, leading to the temptation of overleveraging.

- **Avoidance Strategy**: Utilize position sizing rules to ensure that no single trade can significantly impact your overall portfolio. Determine the maximum percentage of your capital that you are willing to risk on any given trade and stick to it.

6.2 Lack of a Trading Plan

Entering trades without a clear strategy or plan is akin to navigating unknown waters without a map.

- **Avoidance Strategy**: Develop a comprehensive trading plan that includes your trading goals, risk tolerance, criteria for entry and exit, and money management rules. Adhere to this plan rigorously to impose discipline on your trading activities.

6.3 Ignoring the Importance of Time Decay

Time decay (theta) can erode the value of options, particularly as expiration approaches, catching inexperienced traders off guard.

- **Avoidance Strategy**: Be mindful of the expiration dates of the options you trade and how time decay might affect their value. Consider strategies that benefit from time decay, like selling options, as part of your overall approach.

6.4 Underestimating the Impact of Volatility

Volatility can significantly affect options pricing, and misunderstanding its role can lead to unexpected outcomes.

- **Avoidance Strategy**: Educate yourself on how volatility impacts options prices and use tools like the Greeks, particularly Vega, to assess sensitivity. Consider both historical and implied volatility when planning your trades.

6.5 Poor Risk Management

Failing to manage risk properly can result in substantial, sometimes unrecoverable, losses.

- **Avoidance Strategy**: Implement stop-loss orders or mental stop-loss points to limit potential losses. Regularly review open positions to assess whether they align with your current market outlook and risk tolerance.

6.6 Overtrading

The ease of trading options can lead to overtrading, where the compounding of transaction costs and the potential for poor decision-making can erode profits.

- **Avoidance Strategy**: Set clear criteria for trade entry and exit, and resist the urge to trade based on emotions or the need to be "in the market." Quality over quantity should be a guiding principle in your trading approach.

6.7 Neglecting Post-Trade Analysis

Failing to review and learn from past trades, both successful and unsuccessful, can hinder the improvement of your trading skills.

- **Avoidance Strategy**: Maintain a trading journal detailing the rationale for each trade, the outcomes, and any lessons learned. Regularly review this journal to identify patterns in your trading behavior and areas for improvement.

Conclusion

Avoiding common pitfalls in options trading requires discipline, continuous education, and a well-thought-out trading plan. By recognizing and addressing these challenges proactively, you can enhance your decision-making process, manage risks more effectively, and position yourself for long-term success in the options market. Remember, every trader encounters setbacks; the key is to learn from them and adapt your strategies accordingly.

6.1 Overtrading and Emotional Trading

Overtrading and emotional trading are two of the most common pitfalls that can adversely affect options traders. These behaviors not only can diminish returns but also increase risks disproportionately. Understanding the triggers and implementing strategies to mitigate these behaviors are crucial for maintaining a disciplined trading approach.

Overtrading

Overtrading occurs when a trader makes excessive trades beyond what their strategy or trading plan justifies. It often stems from the desire to recover losses quickly or the fear of missing out on perceived opportunities.

- **Causes**: Chasing losses, market FOMO (Fear Of Missing Out), or excessive confidence after a streak of successful trades can lead to overtrading.
- **Risks**: Increases transaction costs, leads to poorer decision-making, and can expose the trader to unnecessary market risks.
- **Mitigation Strategies**:
  - **Adherence to a Trading Plan**: Define clear criteria for entry and exit points, and stick to them.
  - **Set Trading Limits**: Establish daily or weekly limits on the number of trades or maximum capital at risk.

- o **Scheduled Breaks**: Take regular breaks from trading to reassess strategy and market conditions.

Emotional Trading

Emotional trading occurs when decisions are driven by feelings like fear, greed, or hope, rather than rational analysis and adherence to a trading plan.

- **Causes**: Emotional responses to market volatility, personal financial pressures, or the psychological impact of previous trades can cloud judgment.
- **Risks**: Leads to impulsive decisions, such as cutting profitable trades too early out of fear or holding onto losing positions in the hope of a turnaround.
- **Mitigation Strategies**:
    - o **Emotional Awareness**: Recognize and acknowledge your emotional state before making trading decisions.
    - o **Pre-Defined Rules**: Have strict rules for trade management, including stop-loss orders and profit targets, to take emotions out of the equation.
    - o **Mindfulness Practices**: Techniques such as meditation can help manage emotional responses to market events.

Combining Strategies for Effectiveness

Combating overtrading and emotional trading requires a combination of discipline, self-awareness, and a well-structured trading plan. Integrating the following overarching strategies can enhance your trading discipline:

- **Continuous Learning**: Commit to ongoing education about markets, strategies, and psychological aspects of trading to build confidence and reduce emotional decision-making.
- **Use of Technology**: Employ trading platforms with features that can enforce trading limits, automatically execute stop-loss orders, and provide alerts to help maintain discipline.
- **Peer Support and Mentorship**: Engage with a community of traders or a mentor to share experiences, gain perspective, and receive support during challenging times.

Conclusion

Overtrading and emotional trading are significant challenges that can derail even the most experienced traders. By recognizing the signs of these behaviors and implementing structured strategies to mitigate them, traders can maintain a disciplined approach to the market. Remember, successful trading is not just about making profitable trades but also about managing oneself in the face of market uncertainties and emotional pressures.

6.2 Mismanagement of Capital

Capital mismanagement is a critical pitfall that can significantly undermine the success of options traders. Effective capital management involves not only preserving your trading capital but also allocating it judiciously to maximize potential returns while minimizing risks. This section discusses common capital mismanagement issues and strategies to address them, ensuring a sustainable trading approach.

Common Capital Mismanagement Issues

- **Overallocation to Single Trades**: Placing too much capital into a single trade can lead to significant losses, jeopardizing the overall health of the trading account.
- **Failure to Diversify**: Concentrating capital in similar trades or correlated assets increases risk, as adverse market movements can impact multiple positions simultaneously.
- **Neglecting Cash Reserves**: Not maintaining a portion of the portfolio in cash can limit the ability to take advantage of new opportunities or manage unexpected market events.

Strategies for Effective Capital Management

- **Position Sizing**: Implement rules for position sizing to ensure no single trade risks more than a predetermined percentage of your total capital. A common guideline is to risk no more than 1-2% of your trading capital on a single trade.
- **Portfolio Diversification**: Spread your capital across various trades and asset classes to reduce risk. Consider different sectors, financial instruments, and strategies to achieve a balanced portfolio.
- **Cash Reserves**: Maintain a portion of your portfolio in cash or cash equivalents. This reserve acts as a buffer

against losses and provides liquidity for new trading opportunities or to adjust existing positions.

- **Use of Stop-Loss Orders**: Employ stop-loss orders to automatically close out losing positions at predetermined price levels, helping to manage risk and preserve capital.
- **Regular Portfolio Review**: Conduct periodic reviews of your portfolio to assess performance, rebalance as necessary, and ensure alignment with your trading objectives and risk tolerance.

The Role of Leverage

Options inherently provide leverage, allowing for control of a significant amount of assets with a relatively small investment. While leverage can amplify returns, it also increases risk, making prudent capital management even more critical.

- **Leverage Awareness**: Be conscious of the leverage effect in options trading and how it impacts potential losses.
- **Leverage Limits**: Set limits on the amount of leverage used in your trading. Consider the potential for amplified losses and ensure they are within your risk tolerance.

Psychological Aspects of Capital Management

Effective capital management is not only a matter of technical strategies but also psychological discipline.

- **Emotional Discipline**: Avoid the temptation to overtrade or chase losses, which can lead to rapid capital depletion.

- **Long-Term Perspective**: Focus on long-term trading success rather than short-term gains. Sustainable trading practices contribute to lasting success and capital preservation.

Conclusion

Mismanagement of capital can be a significant barrier to successful options trading, but with disciplined strategies and a focus on risk management, it can be effectively mitigated. By adhering to principles of position sizing, diversification, maintaining cash reserves, and leveraging with caution, traders can protect their capital and position themselves for sustainable success. Remember, the goal of capital management is not just to protect your capital but to ensure it is working effectively for you within the bounds of your risk tolerance and trading objectives.

6.3 Avoiding Bad Trades: Tips and Tricks

Navigating the options market successfully involves not just identifying good trading opportunities but also avoiding potentially bad trades. While no strategy is foolproof, certain practices can help minimize the chances of entering unfavorable positions. This section provides actionable tips and tricks to help you discern and steer clear of bad trades, enhancing your trading discipline and decision-making process.

Define Clear Entry and Exit Criteria

- **Objective Criteria**: Establish objective, quantifiable criteria for entering and exiting trades based on

technical indicators, fundamental analysis, or a combination of both. This approach helps remove emotion from decision-making.
- **Pre-Trade Checklist**: Develop a checklist of conditions that must be met before you enter a trade. If the setup doesn't tick all the boxes, reconsider taking the position.

Conduct Thorough Research and Analysis

- **Due Diligence**: Before entering a trade, conduct thorough research on the underlying asset, including recent news, earnings reports, and any macroeconomic factors that could impact its price.
- **Technical Analysis**: Utilize technical analysis tools to identify trends, support and resistance levels, and potential reversal points. Confirm your findings with multiple indicators to increase confidence in the trade.

Use Risk Management Techniques

- **Position Sizing**: Never allocate more capital to a trade than you are willing to lose. Use position sizing to ensure that a single bad trade won't significantly impact your overall portfolio.
- **Stop-Loss Orders**: Set stop-loss orders to automatically exit a position if it moves against you, limiting your potential loss.

Maintain a Trading Journal

- **Record Keeping**: Maintain a detailed journal of all your trades, including the rationale for entering and exiting, the outcome, and any lessons learned.

- **Review and Reflect**: Regularly review your trading journal to identify patterns in your trading, particularly mistakes or assumptions that led to bad trades. Use these insights to refine your trading strategy and avoid similar pitfalls in the future.

Stay Informed and Adapt to Market Conditions

- **Market Awareness**: Stay informed about overall market conditions and be prepared to adapt your strategy in response to changing dynamics. What works in a bull market may not work in a bear market, and vice versa.
- **Continuous Learning**: Commit to ongoing education in trading strategies, market analysis, and the psychological aspects of trading. The more informed you are, the better equipped you'll be to identify and avoid bad trades.

Practice Patience and Discipline

- **No Trade is Better Than a Bad Trade**: Recognize that not trading is sometimes the best decision. If the market isn't presenting clear opportunities that align with your strategy, it's prudent to stay on the sidelines.
- **Emotional Control**: Cultivate the ability to control impulses and emotions. Don't let the fear of missing out (FOMO) or the desire to recoup losses push you into questionable trades.

Conclusion

Avoiding bad trades is as crucial to trading success as executing profitable ones. By establishing clear trading criteria, conducting thorough research, employing risk management techniques, maintaining a trading journal, staying informed, and practicing patience and discipline, you can significantly reduce the likelihood of entering unfavorable positions. Remember, successful trading is not about winning every trade but about making informed decisions, managing risk, and preserving capital to trade another day.

Chapter 7: Your Path Forward

As you navigate the complexities of options trading, it's essential to view your journey not as a destination but as an ongoing process of learning, adaptation, and growth. The final chapter of this guide is designed to set you on a path forward, emphasizing continuous improvement, advanced education, and the development of a resilient trading mindset. Here's how you can continue to evolve as an options trader and refine your approach to achieve long-term success in the markets.

7.1 Continuous Learning and Skill Enhancement

The markets are dynamic, and staying informed is key to maintaining a competitive edge.

- **Educational Resources**: Regularly engage with books, online courses, webinars, and workshops focused on options trading and financial markets to deepen your knowledge.
- **Market Analysis**: Stay abreast of global economic news, market trends, and financial analysis to inform your trading decisions.
- **Advanced Strategies**: As you gain experience, gradually explore more sophisticated options strategies to diversify your trading approach and manage risks more effectively.

7.2 Networking and Community Engagement

Joining a community of like-minded traders can provide support, insights, and new perspectives.

- **Trading Forums and Groups**: Participate in online forums, local trading groups, or social media communities where traders share experiences, strategies, and advice.
- **Mentorship**: Consider finding a mentor who can offer guidance, share experiences, and provide feedback on your trading approach.

7.3 Embracing Technology

Leverage technology to enhance your trading efficiency, analysis, and decision-making.

- **Trading Platforms**: Stay updated with the latest features and tools offered by your trading platform to aid in analysis and execution.
- **Analytical Tools**: Utilize advanced charting software, trading bots, and risk management tools to streamline your trading process and make more informed decisions.

7.4 Risk Management and Psychological Resilience

Continuously refine your risk management practices and develop the mental fortitude required to handle the ups and downs of trading.

- **Risk Assessment**: Regularly review and adjust your risk management parameters to align with your changing financial situation, market conditions, and trading performance.
- **Mindset Development**: Work on cultivating a resilient trading mindset through stress management

techniques, maintaining a healthy work-life balance, and staying disciplined in your approach.

7.5 Performance Review and Strategy Refinement

Consistently evaluate your trading performance and be willing to adapt your strategies as needed.

- **Trading Journal**: Keep a detailed record of your trades, including the rationale, outcomes, and emotional state, to identify patterns and areas for improvement.
- **Strategy Adjustment**: Be open to refining or overhauling your trading strategies based on performance reviews, market changes, and new learnings.

7.6 Setting Long-Term Goals

Define clear, achievable long-term goals for your trading journey to stay motivated and focused.

- **Financial Objectives**: Set specific income or growth targets, along with timelines and milestones to gauge your progress.
- **Personal Development**: Outline goals related to skill development, risk management proficiency, and psychological resilience.

Conclusion

Your path forward in options trading is one of perpetual growth and adaptation. By committing to continuous learning, engaging with the trading community, leveraging technology, and honing your risk management and psychological resilience, you can navigate the markets more effectively and achieve your trading objectives. Remember, success in options trading is not measured by short-term profits but by long-term growth, consistency, and the ability to navigate the complexities of the market with confidence and discipline.

7.1 From Beginner to Advanced: Next Steps

Transitioning from a beginner to an advanced options trader involves a journey of continuous learning, skill development, and practical experience. As you move forward, focusing on deepening your market understanding, refining your strategies, and cultivating a disciplined trading mindset will be crucial. This section outlines key steps to elevate your trading expertise and navigate the path from beginner to advanced.

Deepen Your Market Knowledge

Expanding your understanding of financial markets, economic indicators, and the factors that drive options pricing is foundational to advancing your trading skills.

- **Educational Resources**: Commit to ongoing education through books, courses, and webinars that cover advanced trading concepts, market analysis techniques, and financial theories.
- **Market Analysis**: Regularly analyze market conditions, incorporating both fundamental and technical analysis to inform your trading decisions.

Master Advanced Trading Strategies

Beyond basic calls and puts, advanced strategies can offer more nuanced market positions and risk management options.

- **Spread Strategies**: Become proficient in constructing various spread strategies, such as vertical, horizontal, and diagonal spreads, to exploit different market conditions.
- **Multi-leg Strategies**: Learn to execute complex strategies like iron condors, butterflies, and straddles/strangles, understanding the risk/reward profiles and ideal market conditions for each.

Refine Risk Management Techniques

Effective risk management is even more critical as you engage in complex trades.

- **Position Sizing**: Continuously refine your approach to position sizing, ensuring that each trade is proportionate to your overall risk tolerance and portfolio size.
- **Portfolio Diversification**: Use advanced options strategies not only to seek profits but also to diversify your portfolio, reducing overall risk.

Develop a Robust Trading Plan

A comprehensive trading plan is your roadmap, detailing your strategies, risk management rules, and criteria for evaluating performance.

- **Strategy Documentation**: Clearly document your trading strategies, including entry and exit criteria, risk/reward parameters, and conditions for strategy adjustments.
- **Performance Review**: Incorporate regular performance reviews into your plan to assess what's working, what isn't, and where adjustments are needed.

Cultivate a Professional Trading Mindset

The psychological aspect of trading becomes increasingly important as you advance.

- **Emotional Discipline**: Work on maintaining emotional control, especially in the face of market volatility or when trades don't go as planned.
- **Continuous Improvement**: Adopt a mindset of continuous improvement, viewing losses as learning opportunities and staying open to new strategies and ideas.

Leverage Technology and Tools

Advanced trading platforms and tools can provide deeper insights and facilitate more sophisticated trades.

- **Trading Platforms**: Explore advanced features and analytics offered by trading platforms to enhance your market analysis and execution capabilities.
- **Simulation Tools**: Utilize backtesting and simulation tools to test strategies before deploying them in live markets.

Engage with a Community

Joining a community of experienced traders can provide insights, support, and new perspectives.

- **Trading Forums and Groups**: Participate in trading communities, forums, and social media groups to exchange ideas and strategies with fellow traders.
- **Professional Networks**: Attend trading seminars, workshops, and conferences to network with professional traders and industry experts.

Conclusion

The transition from beginner to advanced options trading is a multifaceted process involving the deepening of market knowledge, mastery of complex strategies, rigorous risk management, and the development of a disciplined trading mindset. By committing to continuous learning, staying adaptable to market changes, and leveraging community and technological resources, you can enhance your trading proficiency and navigate the options market with greater confidence and skill.

7.2 Staying Informed: Continuous Learning

In the ever-evolving landscape of options trading, continuous learning is not just a recommendation—it's a necessity. The markets are dynamic, influenced by global economic events, changing regulations, and technological advancements. Staying informed and committed to ongoing education is crucial for maintaining a competitive edge and adapting to new challenges. This section offers strategies for ensuring that your knowledge and skills remain current and relevant.

Leverage Educational Resources

The wealth of information available to traders today is vast and varied, offering multiple avenues for learning and growth.

- **Books and Publications**: Keep an eye out for new publications and classic texts that delve into advanced trading strategies, market analysis, and financial theories.
- **Online Courses and Webinars**: Take advantage of online platforms offering courses and webinars tailored to options traders at all levels. These can range from intermediate strategies to advanced market analysis techniques.
- **Financial News and Journals**: Subscribe to leading financial news outlets, journals, and magazines to stay updated on market trends, economic indicators, and geopolitical events that could impact the markets.

Participate in Trading Communities

Engaging with a community of traders can provide real-time insights, support, and diverse perspectives.

- **Forums and Social Media**: Join online trading forums, social media groups, and platforms where traders share strategies, experiences, and advice. Being part of these communities can expose you to new ideas and approaches.
- **Networking Events and Conferences**: Attend trading and investment conferences, seminars, and networking

events to connect with other traders and industry professionals. These gatherings can be valuable sources of information and inspiration.

Utilize Analytical Tools and Platforms

Technological advancements have made sophisticated analytical tools and platforms accessible to individual traders, offering deep insights into market behavior.

- **Advanced Trading Platforms**: Explore the advanced features of your trading platform, including market analysis tools, simulation features, and algorithmic trading capabilities.
- **Financial Analytics Software**: Consider using specialized financial analytics software that offers in-depth market analysis, predictive modeling, and strategy backtesting.

Practice Reflective Trading

Reflective trading involves critically assessing your trading activities to identify areas for improvement and adapt your strategies accordingly.

- **Trading Journal**: Maintain a detailed trading journal that not only tracks your trades but also your rationale, market conditions, and emotional state for each trade. Regular review of this journal can highlight patterns and areas for growth.
- **Post-Trade Analysis**: Conduct post-trade analyses to understand what worked, what didn't, and why. This practice can inform future strategies and decision-making.

Embrace a Culture of Adaptability

The ability to adapt to changing market conditions, regulations, and new trading instruments is essential for sustained success.

- **Market Adaptability**: Stay flexible in your strategies and be willing to pivot based on market conditions and emerging trends.
- **Lifelong Learning**: Cultivate a mindset of lifelong learning, recognizing that there is always more to learn and that the markets will continue to evolve.

Conclusion

Continuous learning and staying informed are fundamental to thriving in the dynamic world of options trading. By leveraging educational resources, engaging with trading communities, utilizing advanced tools, practicing reflective trading, and embracing adaptability, you can enhance your trading acumen and navigate the markets with confidence. Remember, the pursuit of knowledge is ongoing, and each step in your learning journey can open new doors to opportunities and success in the trading arena.

7.3 Building a Network of Traders

In the journey of options trading, building a network of fellow traders can be invaluable. A strong network provides not just camaraderie but also a wealth of shared knowledge, diverse perspectives, and mutual support. This section outlines strategies for cultivating a robust trading network, facilitating both personal growth and enhanced market understanding.

Engage in Online Trading Communities

The digital age has made it easier than ever to connect with traders worldwide.

- **Trading Forums and Social Media**: Platforms like Reddit, Twitter, and specialized trading forums host vibrant communities where traders discuss strategies, share insights, and offer support.
- **Webinars and Virtual Meetups**: Attend webinars and virtual meetups hosted by trading platforms, educational institutions, or trading groups. These can be great places to meet like-minded individuals.

Participate in Local Trading Groups

While online communities are valuable, there's also significant benefit in face-to-face interactions.

- **Local Trading Clubs**: Look for local trading clubs or meet-up groups in your area. Meeting regularly can foster stronger relationships and allow for more in-depth discussions.
- **Seminars and Conferences**: Attend trading seminars, conferences, and workshops. These events not only provide learning opportunities but also networking breaks where you can connect with other attendees.

Leverage Social Media and Professional Networking Sites

Social media platforms and professional networking sites offer avenues to connect with traders and industry professionals.

- **LinkedIn**: Create a professional profile highlighting your trading interests and join trading-related groups. Connect with other traders and participate in discussions.
- **Twitter and Facebook**: Follow professional traders, analysts, and financial commentators. Engage with their content and join trading-related groups.

Offer and Seek Mentorship

Mentorship can be a powerful element of your trading network, providing guidance, motivation, and new insights.

- **Seeking a Mentor**: Look for experienced traders who are willing to share their knowledge. Be clear about what you're looking for in a mentorship and what you can bring to the relationship.
- **Becoming a Mentor**: If you have experience, consider mentoring less experienced traders. Teaching others can also deepen your understanding and expose you to new perspectives.

Collaborate and Share Knowledge

True networking involves a give-and-take relationship where all parties benefit from shared experiences and knowledge.

- **Study Groups**: Form or join study groups with traders at a similar skill level to discuss market trends, review trades, and explore new strategies.
- **Collaborative Research**: Partner with others in your network to conduct research on trading strategies, market analysis, or financial models.

Maintain and Nurture Relationships

Building a network is just the first step; maintaining these relationships is key to a lasting and beneficial network.

- **Regular Communication**: Keep in touch with your trading contacts through regular check-ins, sharing interesting articles, or discussing market developments.
- **Reciprocity**: Be ready to offer assistance and support to your network contacts. Networking is most effective when all parties are engaged and willing to help each other.

Conclusion

Building a network of traders enriches your trading journey with collective wisdom, support, and diverse strategies. By actively engaging in both online and local trading communities, leveraging social media, participating in mentorship, collaborating on knowledge-sharing, and nurturing relationships, you can create a vibrant network that supports your growth and success in options trading. Remember, the strongest networks are built on mutual respect, shared learning, and a genuine interest in each other's success.

Appendix A: Glossary of Terms

The world of options trading comes with its own specialized vocabulary. Understanding these terms is crucial for effective communication and decision-making in the market. This glossary provides concise definitions of key options trading terms to enhance your comprehension and fluency in the language of the markets.

Options Trading Terms

- **Option**: A financial derivative that provides the buyer the right, but not the obligation, to buy (call option) or sell (put option) an underlying asset at a specified price (strike price) within a certain period of time or on a specific date (expiration date).
- **Call Option**: A contract that gives the holder the right to buy the underlying asset at a predetermined price within a specified time frame.
- **Put Option**: A contract that gives the holder the right to sell the underlying asset at a predetermined price within a specified time frame.
- **Strike Price**: The price at which the holder of an option can buy (in the case of a call) or sell (in the case of a put) the underlying asset.
- **Expiration Date**: The date on which an option contract becomes void and the rights to exercise no longer exist.
- **Premium**: The price paid by the buyer to the seller to acquire the rights granted by the option.
- **In-the-Money (ITM)**: Describes an option with intrinsic value. A call option is ITM when the underlying asset's price is above the strike price, and a put option is ITM

when the underlying asset's price is below the strike price.

- **Out-of-the-Money (OTM)**: Describes an option with no intrinsic value. A call option is OTM when the underlying asset's price is below the strike price, and a put option is OTM when the underlying asset's price is above the strike price.
- **At-the-Money (ATM)**: Describes an option where the underlying asset's price is equal to the strike price.
- **Volume**: The number of contracts traded in a given period for a specific options contract.
- **Open Interest**: The total number of outstanding option contracts that have not been settled.
- **Assignment**: The notification to an option writer (seller) that the option buyer is exercising the rights of the option contract.
- **Exercise**: The act of the option holder electing to use the rights granted by the option contract to buy (call) or sell (put) the underlying asset at the strike price.
- **Leverage**: The ability to control a large contract value with a relatively small amount of capital, amplifying both potential gains and losses.

Trading Strategies Terms

- **Spread**: An options strategy that involves buying and selling two or more options on the same asset with different strike prices and/or expiration dates.
- **Straddle**: A strategy involving the simultaneous purchase of a call and a put option on the same underlying asset, with the same strike price and expiration date, to profit from significant price movements in either direction.

- **Strangle**: Similar to a straddle, but the options have different strike prices while maintaining the same expiration date.
- **Covered Call**: A strategy that involves holding a long position in an underlying asset and selling a call option on that same asset to generate income from the option premium.
- **Protective Put**: A strategy where an investor purchases a put option on an asset they already own to hedge against potential losses from falling prices.

Risk Management Terms

- **Stop-Loss Order**: An order placed with a broker to buy or sell once the stock reaches a certain price, designed to limit an investor's loss on a position.
- **Position Sizing**: The practice of determining the volume of shares or contracts to buy or sell, based on pre-set risk management criteria.
- **Diversification**: A risk management technique that mixes a wide variety of investments within a portfolio to reduce exposure to any single asset or risk.

Understanding these terms and concepts is foundational for navigating the options trading environment effectively. This glossary should serve as a quick reference guide, aiding in the clarification of terms and enhancing your trading literacy.

Appendix A: Options Trading Resources

To support your journey in options trading, a wealth of resources is available that can provide education, market insights, and practical tools. This appendix lists various resources, including books, websites, software, and communities, that can enhance your understanding and execution of options trading strategies.

Educational Books

1. **"Options as a Strategic Investment" by Lawrence G. McMillan**: A comprehensive guide that covers various options strategies and market insights.
2. **"The Options Playbook" by Brian Overby**: Offers straightforward explanations of more than 40 options strategies.
3. **"Option Volatility and Pricing" by Sheldon Natenberg**: Delves into volatility and its impact on options pricing and strategy selection.
4. **"Trading Options Greeks" by Dan Passarelli**: Focuses on understanding the Greeks and their role in options trading.

Online Courses and Webinars

1. **CBOE Options Institute**: Offers a range of online courses, webinars, and seminars for traders at all levels.
2. **Investopedia Academy**: Provides comprehensive courses on options trading, from basics to advanced strategies.
3. **TD Ameritrade Education**: Features a wide selection of educational content, including webcasts and courses tailored to options trading.

Websites and Analytical Tools

1. **CBOE (Chicago Board Options Exchange)**: Offers educational resources, trading tools, and detailed information on options contracts.
2. **Option Alpha**: Provides free options trading education, tools, and a vibrant community forum.
3. **Barchart**: Features options screener tools, volatility rankings, and strategy-specific data.

Trading Platforms

1. **Thinkorswim by TD Ameritrade**: Known for its robust options trading tools and analytics.
2. **Interactive Brokers**: Offers advanced trading tools suitable for sophisticated options traders.
3. **E*TRADE**: Features user-friendly options trading tools and analysis software.

Trading Communities and Forums

1. **r/options on Reddit**: A community where traders discuss strategies, share insights, and ask questions.
2. **Elite Trader**: An online community that covers a broad range of trading topics, including options trading.
3. **The Options Industry Council (OIC)**: Provides free educational events, tools, and resources for options traders.

Market News and Analysis

1. **Bloomberg**: Offers financial news, analysis, and market data.

2. **Seeking Alpha**: Features stock market insights and financial analysis, including sections dedicated to options trading.
3. **MarketWatch**: Provides market news, analysis, and data, with a section on options trading.

Regulatory Bodies

1. **Securities and Exchange Commission (SEC)**: Regulates and provides information on securities markets, including options.
2. **Financial Industry Regulatory Authority (FINRA)**: Offers investor education and regulatory resources related to trading.

Conclusion

Leveraging these resources can significantly contribute to your options trading education and strategy development. Whether you're seeking in-depth knowledge from books, real-time market data, community support, or practical trading tools, the resources listed in this appendix can provide valuable support on your trading journey. Remember, the key to successful options trading lies in continuous learning, diligent practice, and staying informed about market developments and regulatory changes.

Appendix B: Case Studies and Real-World Examples

Applying theoretical knowledge to real-world scenarios is crucial in options trading. This appendix presents a selection of case studies and examples that illustrate how various options strategies can be employed in different market conditions. These practical insights can help bridge the gap between theory and practice, providing a deeper understanding of how options work and how they can be leveraged for trading success.

Case Study 1: Utilizing Covered Calls for Income Generation

- **Background**: An investor holds a long position in XYZ stock, currently trading at $50 per share. The investor is looking to generate additional income from this holding without selling the stock.
- **Strategy**: The investor decides to write (sell) covered call options with a strike price of $55, expiring in one month, receiving a premium of $2 per option.
- **Outcome**: If XYZ stock remains below $55 by expiration, the call options expire worthless, allowing the investor to keep the premium as income. If the stock exceeds $55, the investor may have to sell the stock at $55 but still benefits from the stock's appreciation and the premium received.

Case Study 2: Hedging with Protective Puts

- **Background**: An investor is concerned about a potential short-term downturn in ABC stock, currently priced at $100, which they hold in their portfolio.
- **Strategy**: To hedge against this risk, the investor buys put options with a strike price of $95, expiring in three months, for a premium of $3 per option.
- **Outcome**: If ABC stock falls below $95, the investor can exercise the puts to sell their shares at the protected price of $95, thereby limiting their downside risk. If the stock does not fall below $95, the maximum loss is the premium paid for the puts.

Case Study 3: Speculating with Long Straddles

- **Background**: A significant earnings announcement is expected from DEF company, and substantial price volatility is anticipated, but the direction of the move is uncertain.
- **Strategy**: The trader buys both a call and a put option at an at-the-money strike price of $75, with both options expiring shortly after the earnings announcement. The call and put options are purchased for premiums of $4 and $3.50, respectively.
- **Outcome**: If DEF stock makes a significant move in either direction following the earnings announcement, one of the options will become profitable enough to cover the cost of both premiums and potentially generate additional profit. If the stock price remains near $75, the trader may incur a loss limited to the total premiums paid.

Case Study 4: Capitalizing on Market Stability with Iron Condors

- **Background**: Company GHI's stock is trading at $200, and the market is expected to be range-bound in the near term due to conflicting economic indicators.
- **Strategy**: The trader establishes an iron condor by selling an out-of-the-money call with a strike price of $210 and buying a further out-of-the-money call with a strike price of $220. Simultaneously, the trader sells an out-of-the-money put with a strike price of $190 and buys a further out-of-the-money put with a strike price of $180. All options have the same expiration date.
- **Outcome**: If GHI's stock price remains between $190 and $210 until expiration, all options expire worthless, and the trader keeps the premiums received for selling the call and put. If the stock ventures outside this range, the trader's losses are capped by the long call and put positions.

Conclusion

These case studies illustrate the versatility of options strategies in different market scenarios, from income generation and hedging to speculation and capitalizing on market stability. By analyzing real-world examples, traders can gain practical insights into strategy selection, risk management, and potential outcomes, enhancing their ability to apply theoretical knowledge to live trading situations. Remember, each trading scenario is unique, and a thorough analysis of market conditions, financial objectives, and risk tolerance is essential before implementing any options strategy.

Index

An index in a book serves as a comprehensive guide, allowing readers to quickly locate information on specific topics, terms, or strategies. In the context of a book on options trading, the index would include key concepts, terms, strategies, and case studies covered throughout the text. Below is a structured representation of what an index for this options trading guide might look like, categorized alphabetically for ease of reference.

A

B

C

D

- Market Analysis, 82, 85
- Moving Averages, 48, 51

N

- Networking, 82, 89, 93

O

- Open Interest, 96
- Option, 53
- Out-of-the-Money (OTM), 7. 96
- Overtrading, 73

P

- Position Sizing, 76, 79, 86, 97
- Protective Puts, 13, 44, 67
- Premium, 7, 95
- Put Option, 6

R

- Risk Management, 9, 36

S

- Sideways Trends, 50
- Spread Strategies, 86
- Stop-Loss Orders, 79
- Straddle Strategy, 65
- Strangle Strategy, 97
- Strike Price, 95

T

- Technical Analysis, 49, 79
- Time Decay, 36, 64
- Trading Communities, 89
- Trading Plan, 86

V

- Vertical Spreads, 59
- Volatility, 71

W

- Webinars, 92

This index is structured to provide quick access to various subjects and concepts discussed in the guide, facilitating easy navigation and reference for readers seeking specific information on options trading.

Ernie Braveboy is a seasoned financial expert and author known for his insightful analysis and expertise in options trading. With years of experience in the financial markets, Ernie has developed a deep understanding of the complexities of options trading, including strategies, risk management, and market psychology.

Ernie's career began with a strong academic foundation in finance and economics, which fueled his passion for the stock market and, more specifically, options trading. His professional journey has spanned various roles within the financial industry, including positions as a financial analyst, trader, and consultant for several prestigious financial institutions. This diverse background has provided him with a well-rounded view of the markets and the challenges traders face.

As an author, Ernie has a talent for demystifying complex financial concepts, making them accessible to traders of all levels. His writings often focus on practical strategies, avoiding common pitfalls, and the importance of a disciplined approach to trading. Ernie is known for his clear, concise writing style, which, combined with his practical insights, has made his books valuable resources for both novice and experienced traders.

Beyond his written work, Ernie is committed to education and mentoring within the trading community. He frequently conducts workshops, webinars, and seminars, sharing his knowledge and experiences to help others achieve their trading goals. His approachable demeanor and ability to connect with his audience have made him a respected figure in trading circles.

Ernie's contributions to the field of options trading extend beyond his written work and public speaking. He is an active participant in various online trading forums and social media platforms, where he engages with other traders, answers questions, and shares market insights. This continuous engagement with the trading community reflects his ongoing commitment to learning and sharing knowledge.

In his personal time, Ernie is an avid reader and enjoys staying abreast of the latest financial news and market trends. He also believes in the importance of work-life balance and enjoys outdoor activities and spending time with family and friends.

Ernie Braveboy's dedication to the field of options trading, combined with his extensive knowledge and willingness to share his expertise, has made him a valued author and mentor in the financial community. His work continues to inspire and guide traders on their journey to success in the options market.

Conclusion

In conclusion, the journey through the intricacies of options trading, from the foundational principles and strategies to the advanced techniques and risk management practices, represents a comprehensive pathway for traders seeking to navigate this complex yet rewarding domain. The guide has endeavored to equip readers with the essential knowledge, practical insights, and strategic frameworks necessary to embark on or enhance their options trading endeavors.

Central to this journey is the recognition of the dynamic nature of the financial markets and the imperative of continuous learning and adaptation. The strategies and insights presented serve not only as a starting point but also as a guide for ongoing development, encouraging traders to remain informed, disciplined, and reflective in their trading practices.

Moreover, the emphasis on building a network of traders, leveraging educational resources, and maintaining a disciplined trading mindset underscores the multifaceted approach required for sustained success in options trading. It is through the amalgamation of technical skills, strategic acumen, and psychological resilience that traders can aspire to achieve their financial objectives and navigate the market's uncertainties with confidence.

As readers forge ahead in their options trading journey, they are encouraged to approach each trade with due diligence, to learn from both successes and setbacks, and to view trading not just as a pursuit of financial gain but as a continuous journey of learning and personal growth. The path forward is one of exploration, adaptation, and steadfast commitment to the principles of sound trading practice.

If you've found value in this guide to options trading, I would greatly appreciate it if you could take a moment to leave a review on Amazon.

Your feedback not only helps me to improve future editions but also assists other readers in discovering resources that can aid in their trading journey.

Sharing your thoughts and experiences with the book can make a significant difference. Thank you for your support and for being part of this learning community!

Preview: "Stock Investing for Beginners in 2023: Maximizing Your Investment Potential: A Guide for New Investors in the Post COVID-19 Economy"

STOCK
INVESTING
FOR BEGINNERS
IN 2023

MAXIMIZING YOUR INVESTMENT POTENTIAL:
A GUIDE FOR NEW INVESTORS IN THE POST
COVID-19 ECONOMY

ERNIE BRAVEBOY

In the ever-evolving financial landscape shaped by the aftermath of the COVID-19 pandemic, "Stock Investing for Beginners in 2023" emerges as a vital guide for those new to the investment world. This book is meticulously designed to navigate the complexities of the post-pandemic economy, offering new investors a solid foundation in stock market fundamentals while addressing the unique challenges and opportunities that have arisen in this new era.

Key Highlights:

- **Understanding the Post COVID-19 Economy**: Gain insights into how the global economy is reshaping after the pandemic, including shifts in market dynamics, emerging sectors, and the impact of governmental policies on investments.
- **Stock Market Fundamentals**: Delve into the basics of stock investing, including understanding different types of stocks, how to read market indicators, and the importance of diversification to minimize risk.
- **Investment Strategies for the New Investor**: Learn about various investment strategies tailored for beginners, focusing on long-term growth, income investing, and the principles of value investing in a fluctuating market.
- **Risk Management**: Equip yourself with effective risk management techniques to safeguard your investments against market volatility, emphasizing the importance of a well-thought-out investment plan.
- **Technological Advancements in Trading**: Explore how technological advancements, such as online trading platforms and financial apps, have transformed

the investment landscape, making stock investing more accessible to beginners.

- **Sustainable and Ethical Investing**: Understand the growing trend of ESG (Environmental, Social, and Governance) investing and how aligning your investment choices with your values can lead to sustainable financial growth.
- **Navigating Market Trends**: Learn to identify and analyze market trends, using them to make informed investment decisions that align with your financial goals and risk tolerance.

"Stock Investing for Beginners in 2023" is more than just a guide; it's a companion for the new investor looking to make informed, confident decisions in the stock market. Whether you're looking to build a robust investment portfolio or simply understand the fundamentals of stock investing, this book provides the knowledge and tools necessary to maximize your investment potential in the post-pandemic economy.

For those ready to embark on their investment journey, the full book is available at: https://a.co/d/cBUwdWX. Dive into this comprehensive guide and take the first step towards becoming a savvy investor in today's dynamic market.

Check Out My Other Books

To explore more insightful books by Ernie Braveboy, including a range of topics from options trading to broader investment strategies, you can visit his Amazon author page. Discover a collection of works designed to equip you with the knowledge and tools needed for success in the financial markets.

Visit Ernie Braveboy's author page on Amazon: Ernie Braveboy's Author Page

Dive into his collection to find resources that resonate with your financial goals and trading aspirations.